350
X

INTERNATIONAL IMPLICATIONS
OF FULL EMPLOYMENT IN GREAT BRITAIN

THE ROYAL INSTITUTE
OF INTERNATIONAL AFFAIRS
London: Chatham House, St James's Square, S.W.1
New York: 542 Fifth Avenue, New York 19

Toronto Bombay
Melbourne Cape Town
OXFORD UNIVERSITY PRESS

INTERNATIONAL IMPLICATIONS OF FULL EMPLOYMENT IN GREAT BRITAIN

By

ALLAN G. B. FISHER

*Price Professor of International Economics
at the Royal Institute of
International Affairs*

London & New York
ROYAL INSTITUTE OF INTERNATIONAL AFFAIRS

First published 1946

PRINTED IN GREAT BRITAIN
AT THE BROADWATER PRESS, WELWYN GARDEN CITY
HERTFORDSHIRE

CONTENTS

PREFACE

THIS book was written by Professor Fisher in close association with a group of economists under the Chairmanship of Sir Geoffrey Vickers. After the theme of the book had been determined in discussion with the group, Professor Fisher prepared the syllabus, and drafted and submitted each chapter to prolonged discussion, revising and often re-writing many passages with a view to emphasizing or meeting points to which members of the group attached importance. Supplementary notes have been added which indicate some of the differences in opinion or in emphasis which have been disclosed by the group discussions. Except as disclosed by these notes, the Group is in general agreement with the book. As several members of the group are in official positions, they are unable to allow their names to be used, and the supplementary notes are also unsigned.

April 17, 1946.

Chapter I

INTRODUCTION

THE closeness of the connection between economic conditions in the United Kingdom and the broader stream of world economic development is a commonplace of the economic historian. The impact of total war, however, not only brings forcibly into the foreground of our consciousness the cumulative effects of trends which, almost unperceived, were already throughout the inter-war period quietly registering their consequences, but also initiates new and more radical changes, economic, technical, and psychological. Their effects may be so far-reaching that we cannot afford to take it for granted without further close examination that traditional views on the significance of this connection need no revision.

Partly as a consequence of the war, the United Kingdom is now committed to two broad economic policy objectives, and, lest there should be any concealed contradiction or inconsistency between them, their full implications should be carefully examined. Internally we are committed to a policy of "full employment". There were some sharp differences of opinion as to the adequacy of the means for achieving this end set forth in the White Paper on Employment Policy of May 1944. But the publication of that document, with the formal acceptance by the Government "as one of their primary aims and responsibilities" of "the maintenance of a high and stable level of employment after the war"[1] may safely be interpreted as proof of a definite shift of the centre of gravity of British opinion in relation to this problem. Around this centre significant variations will no doubt continue to be observed, but the target at which every one, irrespective of party differences, will agree that we should aim will not be the same as the target of the inter-war period.

On the other hand, internationally we are committed, though for reasons of a different kind, to the reconstruction in some

[1] Cmd. 6527, p. 3.

1

form or other of a competitive liberal international economy. The precise nature of the obligations implied in our acceptance of Article VII of the Mutual Aid Agreement, which set forth the conditions on which the final determination of the Lend-Lease benefits received from the United States was to be based, has properly been regarded as a matter for the most careful deliberation, and the question was made no easier by the fact that the obligations assumed were, at least formally, equally binding on economies as diverse in structure and outlook as the United States and the U.S.S.R. But "agreed action . . . directed . . . to the elimination of all forms of discriminatory treatment in international commerce, and to the reduction of tariffs and other trade barriers; and in general, to the attainment of all the economic objectives set forth in the Joint Declaration made on August 14, 1941, by the President of the United States of America and the Prime Minister of the United Kingdom"[1] could scarcely have been interpreted to mean anything else on our part than an effort, so vigorous as to be accepted in the United States as convincing evidence of our good faith, to reconstruct something, which, however qualified or modified, would be recognizable as a "liberal"—or perhaps it would be better to say an "open"—world order. As will be argued later, the United Kingdom has a direct interest of its own in facilitating the restoration of the essential elements of an international economic policy based on these principles, which have served it so well in the past, and the rejection of which would threaten the gravest difficulties for the future. It is not simply a question of deferring to the ineradicable prejudices of a powerful ally. But in many quarters it has been feared that the difficulties might be insuperable, and even to-day, when substantial progress has been made in hammering out a concrete programme by which the "agreed action" postulated in Article VII is to be

[1] In the Atlantic Charter, the President of the United States and the Prime Minister of the United Kingdom stated their intention to "endeavour, with due respect for their existing obligations, to further enjoyment by all States, great or small, victor or vanquished, of access, on equal terms, to the trade and to the raw materials of the world which are needed for their economic prosperity", and affirmed their desire "to bring about the fullest collaboration between all nations in the economic field, with the object of securing for all, improved labour standards, economic advancement, and social security".

made effective, not every one is convinced that the objective aimed at can in fact be attained. Any breakdown would, however, have such serious consequences for the United Kingdom that it may safely be assumed that the most earnest efforts will be made to avoid it. Not the least merit of the programme which from December 1945 we must accept as a directive for our national policy is the satisfactory solution which it provides for the delicate question of an appropriate *quid pro quo* for Lend-Lease benefits. To reopen this question would be highly embarrassing, while the prospects of agreement on international political issues, almost universally accepted as a policy objective of overwhelming importance, could not be rated very high if on either side it were now found impossible to translate the international economic policy to which we are now committed into concrete and workable terms.

For many purposes the two problems whose relations and inter-actions it is the purpose of this study to examine can properly be contrasted as being the one internal or national, the other international. The distinction should not, however, be drawn too sharply. The repeated declarations at recent international conferences, e.g. at Hot Springs in May 1943 and in the Declaration of Philadelphia adopted by the International Labour Conference in 1944,[1] culminating in the pledge embodied in Articles 55 and 56 of the Charter of the United Nations, where the purposes for which member States agree "to take joint and separate action in co-operation with the organization" include the achievement of "high standards of living, full employment, and conditions of economic and social progress and development", offer a plausible justification for the belief that full employment itself is now an international and no longer merely a national problem.

The frequent repetition of high-sounding general principles does not in itself provide any guarantee either of their practical significance, or indeed even that the principles thus emphasized

---

[1] "The Conference recognizes the solemn obligation of the International Labour Organization to further among the nations of the world programmes which will achieve: (*a*) full employment and the raising of standards of living; (*b*) the employment of workers in the occupations in which they can have the satisfaction of giving the fullest measure of their skill and attainments and make their greatest contribution to the common well-being . . . ."

have any clear meaning. But even if we do not press our criticism from these angles, full employment, if it has now become an international problem, is still international with a difference. Article 2 of the Charter of the United Nations gave timid Governments an assurance that "nothing contained in the present Charter shall authorize the United Nations to intervene in matters which are essentially within the domestic jurisdiction of any state", and it may safely be surmised that most Governments will interpret employment policy as falling essentially within their domestic jurisdiction. A problem in relation to which we would like as many countries as possible to move along similar or parallel lines may, if we like, be described as international. But the problems which arise from the interaction of the effects of different national policies upon each other are international in a somewhat different and more profound sense, and it is not in this sense that national full employment has, when practical policy is under consideration, been at all widely thought of as constituting an international problem. It is no doubt true, as Miss Frances Perkins said at the International Labour Conference at Philadelphia, that "the maintenance within each nation of high levels of employment and national income is a matter of international concern". Just as a child born into a wealthy community is normally more fortunate than one born in a poor and backward country, so it is better for us in Great Britain to live in a wealthy and prosperous world rather than one which is poor and depressed. It is equally true, and perhaps even more important, that, whether the "normal" average level is high or not, fluctuations in employment in any economy will often have repercussions upon other economies so far-reaching as to entitle them to regard the internal employment policies of other countries as matters directly relevant to the maintenance of international equilibrium. But even in international conferences it is usually assumed that much the greater part of, if not the whole responsibility for employment policy must and will be borne by the respective national authorities concerned, so that for most practical purposes it is not seriously misleading to maintain the customary distinction between the two aspects of the present study.

4

It is important to recognize that British full employment policy may to some significant extent fail to reach the goal at which it is aimed, unless those responsible for its formulation and administration take some care to ensure that their decisions create no difficult employment problems in other parts of the world. As a rule, however, we more naturally and conveniently think of the relations between our own employment policy and international economic policy in a rather different sense. The importance of these relations is not indeed seriously disputed anywhere in this country. As Sir William Beveridge has put it, "a vigorous demand at home and development of international trade are not alternative policies but the two halves of one policy".[1] But it is not inconceivable that, as the content of the two halves is filled in, certain inconsistencies may be revealed between two sets of claims, both of which are widely regarded as essential and not to be questioned. Some examination of the circumstances in which the two policies might support each other, or in which they might conflict, is therefore necessary if our general post-war policy is to be effectively co-ordinated.

Both full employment and an open international economy are convenient shorthand expressions for groups of objectives generally considered desirable. There is some overlapping between the two groups, but they are not identical. Less conveniently the two shorthand expressions often cover as well not only the ends which it is desired to achieve, but also the methods thought likely to be most efficacious for achieving them, and when ends and means are confused in this way, we may deceive ourselves in discovering contradictions which are not really there. We may hastily assume that the attainment of full employment is inconsistent with the maintenance of a certain type of international economic order, when all that we are entitled to say is that the use of certain techniques for achieving these ends, or perhaps the attempt to push their application beyond certain limits, would land us in contradictions. The question whether other techniques might be substituted, no less effective, but free from these difficulties, then demands further consideration.

[1] Sir William Beveridge, *Full Employment in a Free Society*, London, Allen and Unwin, 1944, p. 211.

However ardent our devotion to either of these ends, it is moreover unlikely that any one would go to the full length of urging us to be willing to sacrifice everything else for its attainment. Few would go so far as the member of the Irish Commission of Inquiry into Banking, Currency, and Credit, who affirmed that "to the attaining and maintaining of a condition of full employment every other economic consideration should be subordinated".[1] Whether the "other things", which it is often implicitly assumed we shall also be able to count on having while we are enjoying the benefits of either full employment or an open international order, should or should not be included in a formal definition of these concepts is perhaps a mere matter of words of no great importance in itself. The practical statesman is, however, obliged to take serious account of these implicit expectations, nor will an academic analysis of either concept have much value if it assumes that, by a rigorous definition which excludes these "other things" from its scope, we can absolve ourselves from the obligation to take them into account in our judgment of the practical significance of the analysis.

In formulating general propositions on these issues, it is moreover often difficult to avoid giving an impression that antitheses are being drawn much more sharply and absolutely than is either intended or warranted by the facts. This difficulty is frequently encountered whenever we try to sum up opinion on some issue of general interest. The importance attached to our two groups of objectives and to their various constituent elements varies with different men and with the same men in different circumstances. There has, for example, been much speculation both as to how far a commitment for full employment necessarily implies the acceptance either of compulsory direction of labour, such as has been practised during the war, or of permanently lower standards of living, and as to the extent to which people in general would willingly accept the practical consequences of these implications. But in the nature of things such speculations can scarcely be expected to lead to a conclusion so firm that it can be applied at all times and under all

[1] Peter J. O'Loghlen, Minority Report No. III, Reports of Commission of Inquiry into Banking, Currency, and Credit, 1938, p. 642.

6

circumstances. If already 95 per cent of the labour force were employed, the ordinary man would probably reject both these implications, even if it could be rigorously demonstrated that only by accepting them could the unemployment percentage be reduced from 5 to 3. He would say, in effect, "if that is what 'full employment' means, then 'full employment' will have to go", or, more probably, the meaning popularly attributed to "full employment" would begin to change. But if unemployment had risen to 50 per cent, the ordinary man might feel so differently as to be prepared to accept both implications without much question. The support which can politically be mobilized in favour of either of our main objectives must necessarily depend on what it costs in terms of other desired objectives, or rather on what it is expected to cost, which is not always the same thing, and the estimates relevant for this purpose will themselves be dependent on conditions which are constantly changing.

Much of this might conveniently be expressed in a different way by saying that both our main problems are at least as much political in their nature as they are economic. The economist can claim no special competence to pronounce on political issues; if, however, he wishes to avoid wasting his time in sterile speculation, he must not exclude from the factual data which form the background of his work such information as is available about the views which the electors, who in the last resort are the masters of the Governments which must take responsibility for policy decisions, have already formed or are likely to form on these issues. The word "political" itself is, in this context, not entirely free from ambiguity. The "political" implications which in making his decisions on these two issues the wise statesman cannot afford to neglect are on rather different planes. In relation to full employment he cannot safely ignore the risk that if he fails to give the electors what they want, and in particular if the full employment which his policy provides turns out to include something to which the electors strongly object, he will, in due course, be ejected from office, and some other statesman put in his place. In relation to international policy, on the other hand, it is his duty to take care that political relations with other countries, which are essential for the safety and welfare of his people, are not allowed to deteriorate so far as to put them in an impossibly difficult situation. To appreciate the urgency of this second political problem sometimes seems to demand rather longer views than the immediately obvious requirements of the first. It is not to be expected that the intensity of feeling of the average man will be equally keen in both cases. One of the most important functions of the statesman is to ensure an adequate harmonization between these two points of view.

The risk that antitheses may be too sharply drawn should also be borne in mind when we come to consider details of practical policy. For many purposes it is convenient to label national policies in terms which permit classification under broad and easily distinguishable categories. But such classifications will seldom accurately represent all the facts. A certain eclecticism has nearly always been a characteristic of our national policy, and there is no reason for expecting that this characteristic will disappear. However radical the modifications introduced into British policy, it is unlikely that it will satisfy 100 per cent doctrinaires of any colour. In practical politics compromises are nearly always inevitable.

There is much to be said for discussing all these issues in a spirit of stern scientific detachment, each national economy being examined without prejudice as merely a significant and interesting specimen of a wider genus, and without any particular attention being paid to the special interests of any one country. It would, however, be unrealistic to pretend that most thinking on these subjects in this country did not take British interests as its starting point. This approach is readily understood by readers in other countries, some of whom indeed would probably be more suspicious of representations emanating from British sources if their authors claimed that from the outset they had nothing but wider interests in view. To make British interests our starting point certainly does not mean that we never see any further than this, if for no other reason than because it soon becomes abundantly clear that British interests themselves cannot be adequately served unless serious attention, which goes far beyond mere politeness, is accorded to the interests of other countries. For historical and other reasons, the British economy has now taken such a peculiar shape that mere prudence obliges those who guide its further development to take much wider views than at first sight might seem to be dictated by a narrow interpretation of British interests. Whatever his natural disposition, a wise Briton can never afford to be thoroughly hard-boiled.

There is in principle no good reason for excluding from consideration on the international side of our analysis any region in any part of the world. British economic interests have always been literally world-wide, so that to regard international as synonymous with world-wide would be quite in harmony with British traditions. Nevertheless it would also be unrealistic to pretend that when we talk about international economic policy we do not now as a rule in the first instance think of our relations with the United States. Already in 1927-8 the United States' share in the consumption of nine of the raw materials and foodstuffs most important in terms of value in international trade was 39 per cent of the total for the fifteen most important commercial nations, while according to the calculations of the Economic Intelligence Service of the League of Nations, it accounted in 1925-9 for 46 per cent of the world's industrial production. During the last twenty years there have been many ups and downs, but the key position which these figures reveal as having then been occupied by the United States will probably, now that the war is over, be found to be even stronger than before. The United States is "the most dynamic and significant factor in world economy".[1] Whether we like it or not, the share of the United States in world production and the volume of its external trade are now so large, and are capable of further growth at such a rapid rate, that the policy of that country is inevitably a matter of first-rate importance for every other part of the world. Particularly in this connection the war has merely accelerated and brought more forcibly before our notice trends which had been clearly visible long before. It would indeed, be a mistake to become so obsessed by

[1] Calvin B. Hoover, *International Trade and Domestic Employment*, New York, McGraw Hill, 1945, p. 132.

b

the "problems" of Anglo-American relations as to suppose that if we could get an agreed compromise between the views of the United States and the views of the United Kingdom we need trouble about nothing else. As an American writer has recently put it, "the foreign trade and financial interests of each extend far beyond the limits set by the markets of the other . . . The willingness of either the United States or the United Kingdom to make concessions to the other's point of view is limited by their uncertainty regarding the policies that may be adopted elsewhere in the world".[1] For the United Kingdom in particular, the effects of post-war adjustments in the economies of continental Europe, including Germany, will have considerable importance, and a well-balanced British policy must take them into account. Even if we were to value lightly the obligations already assumed in this country, and which many people believe should be further extended, for the post-war development of backward areas, any decisions finally taken in regard to this matter too will inevitably have important implications both for employment prospects in Great Britain and for the development of our international trade. Nevertheless, we shall not go far wrong if, at least in the preliminary survey which is all that can be attempted here, we concentrate our attention mainly on the relations between this country and the United States. A satisfactory settlement here would not by itself be enough, but it would carry us a long way, and it is worth noting, as important for both political and economic reasons, that a satisfactory settlement with the United States would almost certainly also be a satisfactory settlement with Canada.

Some understanding of the meaning and implications of full employment and of the essential characteristics of the international economic order which policy in conformity with the obligations imposed by Article VII of the Mutual Aid Agreement is presumably designed to establish, is clearly necessary before we can enter upon a fruitful discussion of the interactions between these two sets of objectives. Our first task,

---

[1] Percy W. Bidwell, *A Commercial Policy for the United Nations*, New York, Committee on International Economic Policy in co-operation with the Carnegie Endowment, 1945, p. 26.

therefore, is to present as clearly as we can the fundamental
ideas involved in each case, bearing in mind throughout that
our purpose is not to expound the theory either of full employment or of an open international system for its own sake, but
only so far as there are risks of the practical consequences of the
adoption of these two policies getting in each other's way.

Chapter II

THE CONCEPT OF FULL EMPLOYMENT

DEFINITIONS OF FULL EMPLOYMENT

IN our current political and economic discussions few phrases have become more familiar than "full employment". The ideas associated with the term undoubtedly dominate political thought not only in Great Britain, but also in many other parts of the world. The most powerful and appealing motives urging us to adopt a full employment policy have sprung from a resolute determination to avoid the widespread and persistent unemployment which disfigured the economic and social life of nearly every country during the Great Depression, but it is also widely and understandably insisted that a modern civilized community should not be content merely with the avoidance of mass unemployment. Economics, like other social sciences, has made some notable advances in recent years, particularly in relation to the influences which determine the level of employment, and the normal consequences of an advance in science is a widening of the range within which we can reasonably hope to be able to control our destinies. The judicious application of the new techniques which are based on these recent advances promises to ensure a degree of stability and evenness of economic development much greater than has been the common experience of recent years.

Despite the lively and legitimate interest which these problems have aroused, it is still not an easy task to set forth in terms likely to be acceptable to everybody the essential elements in the meaning of full employment. It should not be thought inconsistent with a due appreciation of the value of these recent additions to our knowledge, both theoretical and practical, to suggest that a preliminary examination of its meaning may safeguard us against some of the risks of subsequent disillusionment, in case the practical difficulties of administering a full employment policy turn out to be greater than at present we expect. There is now fairly general agreement on the important principle that the government should take some significant measure of responsibility for maintaining a proper level of employment, and this fact itself makes it particularly important to ascertain, with as much precision as possible, just what it is that governments are being asked to guarantee.

The results obtained from an analysis of the meaning of "full employment" might be presented in either of two ways. For some purposes it would be advantageous if, following the writers who have contributed most towards the modern theory of full employment, we were to move towards a rigorous theoretical definition which could then conveniently be used as an instrument for further logical analysis of practical policy. According to Lord Keynes, for example, "we have full employment when output has risen to a level at which the marginal return from a representative unit of the factors of production has fallen to the minimum figure at which a quantity of the factors sufficient to produce this output is available".[1] Elsewhere he defines "full employment" negatively as the absence of "involuntary unemployment", and explains that "men are involuntarily unemployed if, in the event of a small rise in the price of wage-goods relatively to the money-wage, both the aggregate supply of labour willing to work for the current money-wage and the aggregate demand for it at that wage would be greater than the existing volume of employment".[2]

The full significance of such definitions is not, however, always at the first glance immediately obvious, and many would prefer something more concrete and less technical. Of the simpler and apparently more precise type of definition, Sir William Beveridge's, "having always more vacant jobs than men",[3] may be taken as an illustration. Its precision is, however, rather delusive, for the abstract concept of a "job" is in fact much less simple than this popular phrase implies. In any event the current lively interest in full employment arises less from its importance as a subject for academic speculation

[1] Lord Keynes, *The General Theory of Employment, Interest, and Money*, London, Macmillan, 1936, p. 15.
[2] Op. cit., p. 15.
[3] Beveridge, *Full Employment in a Free Society*, p. 18.

issuing in definitions such as those we have quoted than from the general eagerness that it should, with the least possible delay, be made the objective of certain very important parts of post-war governmental policy. It will, therefore, probably be more useful at least in the first instance to endeavour to disentangle in descriptive and perhaps less rigorous terms the group of objectives, which, despite wide diversities of opinion about the priority to be given to the various items in the group, may be presumed to be in the minds of most people when they hear "full employment" discussed.

The results of our effort will, in some respects at least, be inevitably, and perhaps disappointingly, vague and confused. Any one who attempts to draw a picture of a confused state of mind can scarcely himself avoid giving an impression of confusion. A substantial part of the difficulty of elaborating a concrete clear-cut policy in this field, arises precisely from half-conscious divergences of view concerning the relative importance of the elements properly to be included in the concept of full employment. It should therefore be useful to embark upon an inquiry which may bring to the surface some of the ambiguities which popular discussions often allow to remain concealed.

With the exception of a few dissenting voices[1] there is general agreement among the "experts" that, contrary to what one might have supposed was the plain meaning of the words, a promise of "full employment" must not be taken as implying that everybody will be continuously engaged in active work. Lord Keynes explained that "full employment", as he defined it in the terms quoted above, is consistent with the survival of both "frictional" and "voluntary" unemployment. Partly, no

---

[1] The appropriation of a term which already has a perfectly obvious common-sense meaning, and its diversion to a use with quite a different meaning, have been condemned by Professor Pigou, who insists that full employment should be taken as meaning what it literally says, i.e. "that everybody who at the ruling rates of wage wishes to be employed, is in fact employed". He adds that he does not regard the establishment and maintenance of full employment, in this sense, after the war as a practical objective (*Lapses from Full Employment*, London, Macmillan, 1945, pp. 1-2). A captious critic might complain that the insertion of the qualification "at the ruling rates of wage" was itself an unjustifiable gloss upon the literal meaning of the phrase.

doubt, for this reason, some cautious writers have been reluctant to use the term, preferring instead to discuss the conditions of "a high level of employment". In many quarters, however, this caution provokes impatient dissent, though it is unlikely that in practice the results will be very different, whatever terms may be chosen to describe the objective in view. Full employment has now been formally enshrined among the objectives at which the United Nations Organization has been instructed to aim, and this may perhaps be regarded as justifying the general use of the more popular phrase.[1] It should, however, always be regarded as a technical phrase with a technical meaning different in some important respects from that suggested by the obvious interpretation of its words.

We have already pointed out that the attainment of full employment is commonly and rightly regarded as meaning something more than the mere negative avoidance of a repetition of the unhappy experience of the Great Depression. And even if it could be arranged that every one should be continuously engaged in active work, the mere provision of work as such would not generally be accepted as an adequate discharge of the obligation to organize full employment. In the minds of most people the attainment of a satisfactory condition of full employment would require the fulfilment of two further conditions. They would expect also a high degree of continuity of employment, and would insist moreover that employment should be

---

[1] "It is recognized"—according to the Governing Principles offered as a basis for discussion at the International Conference on Trade and Employment proposed in December 1945—"that (*a*) in all countries *high and stable employment* is a main condition for the attainment of satisfactory levels of living, and (*b*) the attainment of *approximately full employment* by the major industrial and trading nations, and its maintenance on a reasonably assured basis, are essential to the expansion of international trade on which the full prosperity of these and other nations depends." The words used here appear to suggest that there is still some divergence of opinion about the most appropriate terminology; the cautious phrases italicized above are unlikely fully to satisfy the most ardent devotees of full employ ment *sans phrase*, who have, for example, made it a ground of criticism o the United States Employment Act of 1946 (cf. *infra*., Chapter IX, p. 133 that it appears deliberately to avoid the use of these words. Professor Calvin B. Hoover on the other hand, states that "'full employment' simply connotes freedom from unemployment caused by economic depression", and claims that this is the sense in which economists all over the world now employ the term (*International Trade and Domestic Employment*, p. 48n.).

found in real work which would be reasonably congenial to those who performed it. A state of full employment would have much in common with the employment situation experienced at the peak of the trade cycle, and the target at which a full employment policy should aim is indeed sometimes described as the maintenance of "continuous boom conditions", not, however, a very happy phrase, for the word "boom" has a certain emotional colour which is better avoided in these discussions, while its use here takes for granted the possibility of an indefinite prolongation of the condition commonly so described, and this possibility has to be established and not merely assumed.

It would certainly be generally assumed that in conditions of full employment any one who lost his job through no fault of his own would, in effect, be guaranteed that a reasonably acceptable alternative would be available for him without undue delay. But while on no interpretation of full employment are changes either of occupation or of the place in which work has to be performed entirely ruled out, it is also often assumed that such changes would be reduced to a minimum. If a large proportion of the working population was obliged to change jobs at frequent intervals, many would only with the greatest difficulty bring themselves to describe the situation as one of full employment, even if the volume of unemployment at all times was very small.

"Reduction to a minimum" is, of course, another question-begging phrase which by itself carries the analysis little further. How far can the limits be expanded before such changes are to be condemned as "unreasonable"? No one believes that change of occupation merely for the sake of change has any value. There may, however, sometimes be important specific policy objectives, which would be more expeditiously and effectively attained by a degree of mobility, which many would find uncomfortable, and would on that account be inclined to describe as "unreasonable". Much of the current discussion of full employment suggests that in such circumstances, there must be no insistence upon more mobility than can be supplied by people who actually like change, even if this means that other important objectives have to be sacrificed, or at least, their attainment seriously retarded. It may be an exaggeration to say that the assurance of universal civil service conditions of employment is assumed to be the proper objective—and indeed, civil service conditions often imply a high degree of geographical mobility—but any government which undertook the obligation of assuring conditions of full employment would be widely regarded as having failed in its duty, unless people in general had, subject to qualifications covering misconduct on the one hand and opportunities for promotion on the other, a fairly firm guarantee of the jobs which they already happened to have. The aversion of many important sections of the population to change of either occupation or the location of their work is commonly believed to be so widespread and deep-rooted that public policy must be moulded to ensure that such movements are not imposed upon people who dislike them. Whether this aversion is so general as is sometimes supposed, may indeed be doubted. Even during the difficult inter-war period, large numbers of people did make changes of either kind, with great satisfaction to themselves and equal benefit to the rest of the economy, while others would have been quite happy to change if the conditions for so doing had been more favourable. If conditions were such as to make it easy to effect without delay changes which were both economically desirable and not uncongenial to those who had to make them, the necessity for further changes of a more unpleasant character might be reduced to a minimum or even, in some favourable circumstances, destroyed altogether.[1]

---

[1] An incidental point of some interest, which can only be noted in passing, in a sense raises issues of exactly the opposite kind to those suggested by the claim for the generalization of civil service conditions of employment. What is to be the position in a full employment economy of the small, but not entirely negligible group of marginal people who do not mind taking a job occasionally, but who are temperamentally averse to regular employment? Should we in a free society maintain "the right to be unemployed" which has hitherto been implicitly asserted and practised by the members of this group? To a considerable extent they have so far escaped the attention of the collector of unemployment statistics. If account is to be taken of them in a more far-reaching system of social security, and if we decide that on balance the advantages to be gained from attempting to dragoon them into regular employment would be out of proportion to the trouble which this attempt would involve, we should perhaps be prepared to allow a somewhat wider margin of normal unemployment in a full employment economy than some of the estimates quoted below would permit.

17

The bearing of such implied guarantees on the opportunities to be afforded to new entrants into an occupation or industry is an important point which remains somewhat obscure. For a person entering the labour market for the first time, there can be no "job which he already happens to have", and which can therefore be guaranteed to him. But how much freedom is to be allowed in choosing the niche in the structure of production which henceforth, is to be assured to him? At any point of time the prevailing economic and social institutions give in effect a practical answer to this question. But if guarantees are to be given of greater security of employment than in the past, it becomes necessary to inquire how far prevailing institutions are likely to be satisfactory in the future. Nor can the consideration of this question be safely deferred as raising long-term issues less urgent than the immediate determination of the proper interpretation of the "right to work" as it is to be applied to those already in the labour market. For the introduction of new entrants to active employment is a continuous process. The structure of the labour force even twelve months ahead, and much more five or ten years hence, will be materially affected by the decisions made to-day, about the direction to be taken by the individuals currently entering the labour market. We may reasonably hesitate about giving guarantees of continuous employment twelve months or five years hence, unless we are at the same time satisfied that the stream of labour to whom employment is now being given is not being wrongly directed.

When all these considerations are borne in mind, we cannot do other than agree with the view that "the difficulty of *defining* full employment in any way which is suitable for practical application" is very great,[1] if not indeed quite insuperable, and no convincing quantitative estimate can be offered of the exact meaning of "high" in the phrase, "a high level of employment". One American writer asks for a guarantee that "unemployment, aside from seasonal fluctuations, would never be permitted to exceed 4 per cent of the total labour force."[2]

[1] G. D. N. Worswick, *Economics of Full Employment*, Institute of Statistics, 1944, p. 79.
[2] Stanley Lebergott, "Shall we Guarantee Full Employment?" *Harper's Magazine*, February 1945, p. 200.

More ambitiously Sir William Beveridge maintains that no reasonable approximation to "full employment" will have been maintained if the percentage of unemployment (in which he includes seasonal unemployment) is allowed to rise above 3.[1] A parallel Australian estimate would permit 4 per cent of unemployment among males, but only 2 per cent among females.[2] All such quantitative estimates are inevitably infected by a high degree of arbitrariness, and if the varying degrees of accuracy displayed by unemployment statistics in the past are borne in mind, it may be surmised, without undue cynicism, that any government which assumes a responsibility for maintaining full employment will, in practice, probably be content if it succeeds in avoiding that level of unemployment, whatever it may happen to be, which there is good reason to fear may provoke an inconvenient restlessness among the electorate.

The content of the work to be undertaken must necessarily be taken into account in forming our picture of full employment, but we should equally deceive ourselves if we were to imagine that the remuneration paid for the work performed could safely be dismissed as of little importance. The further question must therefore be examined, to what extent should considerations of real income and standards of living be included in our picture of full employment, however attained? An adequate discussion of the issues raised by this question should be preceded by some examination of the techniques which it is proposed to apply for the attainment of full employment. For our purposes it is more convenient to defer this examination until the next Chapter, but in the meantime we may usefully proceed here with a treatment of the question on broad lines.

FULL EMPLOYMENT AND LIVING STANDARDS

Many of the more popular discussions of full employment have implied, and sometimes specifically asserted that its maintenance will necessarily ensure at the same time the maintenance of customary standards of living. One American writer,

---

[1] Beveridge, *Full Employment in a Free Society*, paras. 167-170.
[2] H. C. Coombs, *Problems of a High Employment Economy*, Joseph Fisher Lecture, June 29, 1944, p. 26.

for example, describes full employment as "a state of affairs in which all men and women willing and able to work will always have the opportunity to do so, at prevailing rates of pay and under prevailing hourly specifications and working conditions generally."[1] Similarly, Sir William Beveridge declares that the jobs to be provided are to be "at fair wages, of such a kind and so located that the unemployed man can reasonably be expected to take them."[2] And another recent writer has been still more downright in defining full employment as "such a state in which everybody who wants work can find it at established rates of pay."[3]

On the other hand, many have applauded "the abandonment of maximum wealth as the test of what is economically desirable",[4] a doctrine which seems to imply not only that a conflict between improvements to living standards and greater security of employment is possible, but also that in such an event the former should be sacrificed to the latter. And while conclusions based upon a meticulous examination of the wording of international documents in which many hands have played a part may be misleading, the fact that higher living standards and a high and stable level of employment are often set forth in official statements as co-ordinate objectives of policy[5] suggests that in many minds the two things are distinguishable and that the one does not necessarily imply the other.

If it is widely assumed that the means used to assure full employment will at the same time necessarily offer adequate safeguards for the protection of standards of living, the question whether the maintenance or improvement of customary standards of living is or is not to be included in a formal definition of full employment is merely a matter of verbal convenience, in itself of no great importance. But we cannot in these circumstances exclude standards of living from our discussion merely

[1] John H. G. Pierson, "An Economic Policy to Insure Permanent Full Employment", *Antioch Review*, 1942.

[2] Beveridge, *Full Employment in a Free Society*, p. 18.

[3] Foreword to *The Economics of Full Employment*, p. iii.

[4] E. H. Carr, *Conditions of Peace*, London, Macmillan, 1942, p. 68.

[5] Among the purposes of the International Monetary Fund, for example, whose constitution was drawn up at Bretton Woods, there are included "the promotion and maintenance" not only "of high levels of employment" but also of "real income".

by defining full employment in narrow terms which make no reference to them. There is a widespread and indeed natural feeling in many countries that something at least as good as the standard of living to which people have been accustomed "must" be assured to them in the future, and where this feeling is strong, there is often a great reluctance to admit that in any conceivable circumstances the attainment of full employment might delay the enjoyment of standards of living regarded as natural. Unfortunately, harmony between full employment policies and the realization of rising living standards cannot be regarded as so inevitable or axiomatic as to make superfluous and unnecessary in an exposition of full employment any reference to the possibility of declining standards.

The phrases which we have quoted above from authors who define full employment as including the maintenance of customary rates of pay, are not entirely free from ambiguity. Stability of money income does not necessarily ensure a corresponding stability of real income, and those who use these phrases may feel themselves free to plead that their claims are still valid even if the means whereby full employment is to be attained include a rising price level which will lower the living standards of some sections of the community. In the abnormal conditions of wartime hyper-full employment, "established rates of pay" have often been maintained with little difficulty, but their maintenance has not always sufficed to ensure the retention of customary pre-war standards of living. Some measure of inflation plays a part of some importance in most of the current full employment programmes, and in view of the well-known tendency for both wage-earners and others to be more insistent, at least in the first instance, about the protection of traditional money-incomes than about the translation of these incomes into real terms, the expectation that such a trend may provoke no serious discontent is not unwarranted. But if prices continue to rise, there is also often a strong pressure to insist that wages should be adjusted accordingly, so that real incomes may not be impaired. Full employment programmes usually, therefore, also insist upon the importance of keeping wage movements under control. The pressure to raise money-wages under conditions of mild inflation may, in the course of time, merge in a struggle for a general re-distribution of income to the advantage of the wage-earners. But especially in Great Britain the wage-earner is usually and naturally most sensitive to changes which threaten to whittle away his customary standard of living, and it is the protection of these standards rather than any improvement in his relative position as compared with other income groups which he usually has in mind in pressing for higher nominal wages. It is the normal and understandable complaint that when prices rise, wages are slow in following their movement. For the most part, therefore, the upward movement of wages which the administrators of a mildly inflationary full employment policy will be anxious to damp down will be an expression of the natural desire of wage-earners to protect their customary standards of living, and to that extent we are justified in saying that the fear that wages may get out of hand is only another way of saying that the real incomes of many wage-earners are expected to fall, and that the conditions necessary for the maintenance of full employment by the means envisaged in these programmes will not easily be assured unless, somehow or other, wage-earners can be persuaded to accept the decline as reasonable.

Just how far this situation has been generally understood by those most intimately concerned is a matter upon which some doubt may legitimately be entertained. Lord Keynes has stated that "it is true, of course, that any increase in employment involves some sacrifice of real income to those who were already employed."[1] Popular expectations upon this subject are, however, probably much more in harmony with Mr Kaldor's view that the increase at the average of $1\frac{1}{2}$ per cent in real income per man-hour which has been a historical fact in the development of the British economy since at least the beginning of this century, will not only continue in the post-war era, but will be greatly accelerated under a full employment policy.[2] It is true that the conditions to which Lord Keynes' thesis applies are those of a static economy, in which increases of productivity

[1] Keynes, *General Theory of Employment, Interest, and Money*, p. 81.
[2] Beveridge, *Full Employment in a Free Society*, pp. 395-7.

are not taken into account, and he was certainly not unaware of the historical trend which is the foundation of Mr Kaldor's optimistic forecast. The extrapolation of historical trends into the future is, however, always a risky business, and at a time when we are being rightly urged to face the possibility that fundamental changes in currently accepted economic practice may be necessary, we may reasonably hesitate if we are asked to assume that trends which operated before any of these changes are made will necessarily be prolonged for our benefit. Especially in those economies where it was most noticeable, the favourable trend of the past was dependent upon a high degree of flexibility, and if full employment policies are not careful to ensure that at least similar high standards of flexibility are maintained, the trends of the future might assume quite a different character.

An unemployed person does not, by the mere fact of being unemployed, cease to be a consumer. Any contribution which he can make to the national output might, therefore, reasonably be regarded as a net gain, and as in a well-ordered community there is little serious risk that the assurance of steady employment will diminish the efficiency of labour, it might at first sight seem a little paradoxical to suggest that measures to increase the volume of employment could, in any circumstances, damage the national income, and thus lower the average *per capita* income level. The alternative situations which we ought to compare are not, however, if our interest extends beyond the immediate future, so simple as this argument suggests. The comparison which it is most important to make is not between two hypothetical national incomes, measured according as we assume that at any given time certain persons are either employed or unemployed, but rather between possible national incomes at some date in the future after our economy has responded to one or other of a number of policies offered for our acceptance to-day. The means chosen to-day for the organization of additional employment are a factor directly relevant to the level of national income to be attained to-morrow. One choice might facilitate the enjoyment of the benefits of greater productivity postulated by Mr Kaldor, while another might condemn us to a level of income substantially lower. If we insist on making the fullest use to-day of all our possibilities of production, we may by so doing render more difficult or even impossible subsequent improvements in our productive resources which would shortly permit a still higher level of output than is possible to-day. "A system—any system, economic or other—that at *every* given point of time fully utilizes its possibilities to the best advantage, may yet, in the long run, be inferior to a system that does so at *no* given point of time, because the latter's failure to do so may be a condition for the level or speed of long-run performance."[1]

No one need, indeed, fear that there is any necessary or even probable incompatibility between the maintenance of high levels of employment and the enjoyment of high standards of living. But we cannot afford simply to take it for granted, as is so often done, that, if full employment is assured by whatever means, high and even rising standards of living will automatically follow. Unfortunately a conflict is quite possible, though happily by no means certain.

The narrower the limits within which we regard it as "reasonable" to expect productive resources to be mobile, the greater are the risks that the attainment of full employment will so strengthen the resistance to the structural adjustments without which higher levels of real income are unattainable that further economic progress may be gravely impeded. We may, for example, quickly approximate to a condition of full employment by a liberal recourse to public works. But if the real cause of the trouble is to be found in monopolistic controls of certain sectors of the labour market, the attainment of higher standards of living would necessitate an approach to full employment by a slower method. It is a matter of the greatest importance to make sure that we select the correct methods for maintaining the level of employment, if in achieving this end the alternative objective of rising standards of living is not to suffer.

Some of the more important illustrations of this point arise precisely in the field with which this study is particularly con-

[1] J. Schumpeter, *Capitalism, Socialism, and Democracy*, London, Allen and Unwin, 1943, p. 83.

cerned, the possibility of a clash between internal and international trade policy. For if, as is widely believed, the implementation of full employment in certain not improbable circumstances may necessitate a rather rigid limitation of imports into this country, the damage done by such restrictions to the British standard of living may, in view of the peculiar structure of our traditional import trade, be quite substantial.[1] Nor would the maintenance of our national income at some agreed appropriate level, measured in monetary terms, necessarily afford any protection against these losses.

The global estimates of national income which are often used in studies of full employment should, indeed, be interpreted with some caution. They are inevitably expressed in money terms, and though the value of the statistical inquiries which have recently been so vigorously prosecuted in this field cannot be questioned, it may be feared that they have sometimes unintentionally diverted attention from the much more important problem of changes in real income. For many important purposes it is worth recording, for example, that the net national income of the United Kingdom increased from £4,604 millions in 1938 to £8,172 millions in 1943, that of Australia from £A788 millions in 1938-9 to about £A1,300 millions in 1943-4, that of Germany from RM. 58·6 thousand millions in 1935 to RM. 77 thousand millions in 1938. But these figures provide only a most imperfect impression of the movements of real income which were going on during the periods under survey, and hypothetical figures of the same kind which forecast national incomes to be attained in the future suffer from a similar defect. It is easy enough to predict that, in certain specified circumstances, national income will reach the level of £x millions, and, if we have sufficient confidence in our index-number technique we may venture to "correct" our estimates

[1] There are obvious and striking differences between the economic structures of the United Kingdom and of Australia, but there is also sufficient similarity to make it relevant to remind the British reader of the view recently expressed by an Australian authority, that "a policy of high employment in an economy so dependent on export trade as is the Australian economy, should not be confused with the maintenance of the prevailing standard of living in all circumstances" (D. B. Copland, *Report on Economic Conditions in the United Kingdom, United States of America, and Canada*, 1945, p. 24).

for price changes, and thus to compare this figure with the national income £y millions recorded for some earlier or later date. But if our £x millions includes a considerable number of items whose statistical significance in the national income is determined merely by the fact that a certain amount of money has been spent in producing them, and if further the hypothetical policy assumed in making our predictions for the future necessitates the exclusion from our real national income of certain other items which many people would have been very glad to buy if they had been available, the comparison may lose much of its significance. The elector may, indeed, be satisfied after the war to be assured a money income which will place him in command of a collection of real commodities and services substantially different from those which he was accustomed to enjoy in 1939. Consumption habits have inevitably been modified during the intervening period, and those who now have no clear recollection of what a banana is like may not feel the permanent loss of such luxuries to be a very serious matter. It may, nevertheless, be dangerous to assume without further question, that the elector will be quite content to accept the products of communal expenditure in large part determined for him according to so-called principles of "social priority" as a permanent substitute for the ordinary things which he was formerly able to buy, but from which he has been temporarily cut off. For in the long run it is of much less interest to him to be assured of a regular money income of £x per annum than to be able, whatever his money income may be, still to buy in the same volume as before the goods and services to which he has become accustomed.

This difficulty is, indeed, only one illustration of the complexities inherent in any careful attempt to give precise meaning to the concept of an average standard of living. When fears are expressed that certain types of full employment policy may threaten a lower standard of living for some important sections of the population, as a result, for example, of an upward movement of prices to which money incomes are not adjusted, the reply is frequently made that this need occasion no concern, for the incomes received by those hitherto unemployed will certainly be large enough to keep the average up. But even if it could be demonstrated that the arithmetic of this argument was irrefutable, and the administrators of full employment found no difficulty in maintaining a satisfactory average, their political embarrassments might still be serious if they were obliged to impose some decline in living standards upon some sections of the community whose support was necessary for them. This is not entirely or even mainly a simple question of the redistribution of income as between rich and poor, for the losses of real income attributable to rising prices might fall heavily upon many people in the lower income groups. Nor can the concern of those who suffer loss be roughly brushed aside as nothing more than an evidence of their unwillingness to subordinate their own selfish interests to the general welfare. If they could show that there was an alternative, though perhaps a slightly slower method, of raising employment to a proper level, which placed more emphasis upon the expanded production of goods at lower cost, and less upon the beneficial effects of a mild inflation, they might, even on the highest grounds of morality, be quite entitled to press their case. At least we should avoid placing too much reliance upon methods which sometimes seem to assume that real incomes can safely be whittled away without any one taking notice of the fact.

LONG-TERM POLICY AND POST-WAR ADJUSTMENTS

The direct significance of these points for British policy in the immediate future is peculiarly difficult to isolate and measure, for nowhere more than here is it so clearly necessary to deal at the same time both with long-term adjustments and with the immediate difficulties of transition from an economy of peace. Radical changes have, in any event, to be made in the structure of an economy which has been grossly distorted by the requirements of war, and these changes must be simultaneous with those required if firm foundations are to be laid for permanent full employment. In certain respects, and especially from the point of view of the mere provision of employment, this may indeed make our immediate task a little easier. For some time to come there will be so many urgent unsatisfied needs, that we may appear to be more seriously threatened by shortages of labour than by unemployment.

The immediate difficulties of Great Britain will, however, also have some impact upon current standards of living. It would be too optimistic to expect that pre-war standards can at once be restored. While the losses of war are being repaired, and the deterioration of productive equipment made good, we shall probably in any case for some time have to content ourselves with something less than this. If, moreover, their restoration is delayed for any substantial period, it will be a delicate task to disentangle the effects of war losses from the effects of any measures which may be adopted to keep up the level of employment. In the meantime also public tastes may so change as to render any direct comparison between current standards of living and those of the pre-1939 period less and less meaningful. It would certainly be unfair to regard full employment policy as solely or even mainly responsible for any decline in real incomes which during the next few years we may find ourselves obliged to accept. But the possibility also cannot be entirely neglected that for some economic and social groups the use in unsuitable circumstances of certain kinds of full employment technique or the attempt to press them further than is warranted by the facts of the current situation, may not at least postpone the time when pre-war standards will again be available for them.

Unanimity in regard to this complex of issues is unlikely to be reached in any near future. In the meantime, we cannot regard any analysis of full employment as adequate which fails to give due consideration to the possibility that certain methods for maintaining full employment may disappoint the widespread expectations that improvements in living standards will be guaranteed at the same time.

It would be quite wrong to assume, as some people are apt to do, that to draw attention to some of the points covered in this analysis of full employment is an indication of a certain lukewarmness about either the urgency of the problem or the efficacy of the methods for dealing with it which have recently become most popular. As is, however, clearly illustrated by the enthusiasm aroused by professions of allegiance to "full employment", as contrasted with the apparently more modest objective of a high and stable level of employment, current popular discussion of this theme is frequently carried on in a quasi-mystical atmosphere which is sometimes unfavourable to clarity in either thought or expression, and in these circumstances some solid advantages might be expected from a sober and detached examination of what full employment really means.

Those who believe that they have discovered an infallible remedy for unemployment may be a little impatient when they are asked to pause and consider this question, or when it is suggested that as a result of their eagerness to push ahead with the detailed elaboration of the remedies to which they attach most importance they may have overlooked certain defects or inadequacies in their programmes of reform. These programmes are frequently presented in a way which suggests the presence in the minds of their sponsors of a strong element of faith to reinforce the conclusions drawn from the processes of rational analysis. In principle, there can be no objection to this; no policy is likely to be successful if those responsible for carrying it out are half-hearted about it. But, however valuable or even necessary an atmosphere of enthusiasm may be for generating the drive and energy without which a merely academic programme may falter and come to grief, it also carries with it the risk of neglecting other elements in the situation which happen to arouse little popular interest, but may nevertheless be quite fundamental. In some of its propagandist aspects, some of the current discussion of full employment is a little reminiscent of the fashions of medical therapy. Some new and valuable techniques have recently been discovered, but some enthusiastic popularizers of these techniques have been too easily led to forget or even to decry the value of the older discoveries of medical science, or to press for the application of the new knowledge in circumstances which are not suitable for them. Those who have themselves taken an active part in building up the body of fundamental knowledge upon which the new techniques are based are, it is interesting to note in passing, usually less liable to errors of this kind.

If, therefore, we recall the value of the older discoveries, we are not necessarily guilty of lack of faith in the new techniques. It is by a judicious combination of the two, with due regard to relevant variations in conditions, that in either case we are most likely to make solid progress towards that condition of general health and well-being, individual and social, which is so much to be desired. For the practical statesman, the central problem is that of determining the appropriate proportions in which the various elements of the programme are to be combined. The tepid interest evinced in many quarters in anything not readily recognizable as a new contribution to the solution of employment problems justifies, however, a persistent insistence that other vital factors should not be at best merely politely recognized, and then for most practical purposes left on one side.

Chapter III

HOW IS FULL
EMPLOYMENT TO BE MAINTAINED?

THIS is not the place in which to attempt to elaborate in any detail a programme for full employment, either in general or for Great Britain in particular. There is already a large and rapidly growing literature on the subject, but as our interest is confined to the narrower question of the relation between full employment and an international economic order, we are justified in ignoring here those parts of the current discussion which have little or no bearing upon that question. We have, however, already suggested that much of the concern sometimes felt about the risks of contradiction between the requirements of our two objectives may be based upon an overhasty assumption that there is only one path leading to the attainment of full employment. If there should be more than one path, these risks might conceivably be diminished or even destroyed by varying the technique which we choose for the attainment of our objective.

It is, therefore, appropriate to say something here about the methods for the maintenance of full employment which have been most seriously considered. The range which might be covered is extremely wide. Already there are some indications that, as so often happens, the wide popularity which the objective of full employment now enjoys may induce the sponsors of every conceivable type of policy to claim full employment as at least one of its by-products. Even if we limit our survey to a consideration of the more serious proposals which are directly and avowedly aimed at the assurance of full employment, there are still many important aspects of the subject with which we need not here concern ourselves. Many of the details around which the most lively controversy has centred we may legitimately neglect, as being merely variants of certain broad principles. Their application in particular cases will, moreover, naturally depend in large measure upon historical accidents

31

and other circumstances which make it quite proper to work out the principles, in the background of the economy of the country in which we happen to be most interested, along lines rather different from those which might more readily come to mind elsewhere.

Our concern here is therefore primarily with broad principles, and not with the details of current controversy, highly important as many of them are. But even after we have thus freed ourselves from the complications of detail, it is still not easy to discover a single basis of logical classification to which we can steadily adhere throughout the analysis. There is an important distinction between techniques which involve the direct action of state instrumentalities in the process of economic development and those which rely more upon the response to various stimuli of individuals and business firms. The distinction between techniques which are primarily fiscal, and those which place more emphasis upon stimuli of a different character is, however, no less fundamental, and classifications based upon these two distinctions will, to some extent, overlap. In the analysis submitted here we shall therefore not attempt to conform to strict principles of formal logic.

MAINTENANCE OF AGGREGATE EXPENDITURE

The first of the "three essential conditions" laid down in the British White Paper on Employment Policy of May 1944 is that "total expenditure on goods and services must be prevented from falling to a level where general unemployment results."[1] The fiscal approach to the fulfilment of this condition leads broadly to two different (though not, of course, contradictory or mutually exclusive) conclusions, according as emphasis is placed upon the maintenance of consumer expenditure by more or less direct means, or upon the more indirect effects of the maintenance of investment at an adequate level. Consumer expenditures may be raised or maintained in the short run by special types of tax adjustment or of transfer payments, or in the long run by more fundamental changes in taxation, social security, wage or agricultural policy. One of the

[1] Cmd. 6527, p. 15.

White Paper proposals, "a scheme for varying, in sympathy with the state of employment, the weekly contribution to be paid by employees and employed under the proposed new system of social insurance,"[1] is a cautious example of action which falls into this category, but other writers, in both Great Britain and the United States, have proposed much more far-reaching action along these lines.

The investment approach usually postulates a tendency, sometimes thought to be so ineradicable as to produce a chronic deficiency of demand, for the volume of private investment to fall below the level necessary for the maintenance of full employment. Whether or not this tendency is ineradicable, there are obviously from time to time fluctuations in private investment, which carry with them, both directly and indirectly, serious unemployment risks. Four main types of proposal for dealing with these fluctuations, types which also are not necessarily contradictory or mutually exclusive, may be conveniently distinguished.

First, inducements may be offered to private business to expand or maintain the level of private investment by policies of "cheap money" or by taxation reforms designed to reduce to a minimum the restrictive effects of taxation upon the expansion of production and employment. Secondly, efforts may be made to co-ordinate or control the investment programmes of private firms with a view to smoothing out some of the fluctuations in activity which are likely if business units are left free to act upon their own independent judgments of the most appropriate time for expansion or for slowing down production. Thirdly, as any benefits anticipated from policies adopted under either of the two previous headings are, as a rule, unlikely by themselves to be adequate to produce the desired result, full employment programmes usually include proposals for an expansion, at the appropriate times, of government expenditure upon goods and services, by public investment, sometimes visualized along lines similar to those of the familiar pre-war public works, but also often elaborated in terms which contemplate a very great extension of direct governmental action in

[1] Cmd. 6527, pp. 22-3.

many parts of the economic field. Finally, as there is a *prima facie* case for the belief that monopoly controls, whether of capital or of labour, impede the expansion of employment opportunities, efforts may be made to expand the volume of employment by limiting or destroying these controls and their effects. Under this heading may be included anti-trust and monopoly control legislation, measures for checking the limitations upon entry into certain occupations sometimes imposed by trade unions and professional bodies, and educational reforms designed to widen some of the bottlenecks which check industrial expansion by limiting the supplies of certain types of skilled labour.

All proposals for maintaining the general level of employment by keeping up the aggregate volume of expenditure are open to an obvious criticism, to which attention has often been directed. Labour is not a homogeneous entity, all parts of which are easily substitutable for each other. It is often highly specialized, and even when specialization has not gone very far, there are always limits beyond which it is impossible for an individual to take up work different from that to which he has become accustomed. Even in the worse times, unemployment is not evenly distributed over all industries and trades, so that while "allowing more purchasing power to remain in the hands of the public will certainly increase the demand for a great variety of goods and services . . ." there is no certainty or probability that this additional demand will exert itself just in those directions in which unemployment is to be found.[1] If coal-mining or shipbuilding is very depressed, no general expansion of purchasing power most of which will be spent on food or clothing or household equipment, will do very much to diminish unemployment among coal-miners or shipbuilders.

FLEXIBILITY OF PRODUCTIVE RESOURCES

To some extent, we may be obliged just to accept as unpleasant realities the difficulties created by these inescapable facts, which indeed, provide the foundation for the most persuasive arguments for social security measures of a more

[1] Beveridge, *Full Employment in a Free Society*, p. 185.

liberal kind than most economies have hitherto been accustomed to provide. We can, however, scarcely be content merely to register the facts and do nothing further about them. The transfer of labour from one employment to another may sometimes be literally impossible. Often, however, it is merely inconvenient, and many full employment programmes accordingly include provision for diminishing the inconveniences of transfer, or for positive inducements to encourage movement out of depressed industries. The White Paper has laid down as a third "essential condition" that "there must be a sufficient mobility of workers between occupations and localities", and the acceptance of this principle also leads to a wide variety of practical proposals. Some schemes are content to wait until unemployment occurs, and then to rely upon organized retraining. A more efficient organization of labour exchanges might also play a useful part.[1] During the war, mobility has often been imposed by positive direction of labour into approved employment, and though anything resembling "forced labour" is naturally unpopular, the preservation of this technique, perhaps in some modified form, is not excluded from some full employment programmes.

Other schemes aim at a greater degree of foresight, and would endeavour to ensure beforehand that the disabilities often associated with transfer from one kind of work or from one place to another should not be unnecessarily oppressive. The educational reforms mentioned above, and indeed the whole range of anti-monopoly measures, might properly be regarded as part of a programme for ensuring greater mobility. It is of little use for people to be willing to transfer from one occupation

[1] The International Labour Office has recently given a good deal of attention to techniques favourable to the more expeditious location of workers in the employment most suitable to them, and detailed suggestions may be found in the Employment (Transition from War to Peace) Recommendation and the Employment Service Recommendation adopted by the Philadelphia Conference of 1944. It is in the broadest sense of the term an international interest that these techniques should be as widely applied as possible, but as the objective of these Recommendations is merely the adoption by national governments of similar or parallel policies, and the problem of the interaction of national policies arises, if at all, only in a very subordinate and relatively unimportant way, we need not in the present study pursue the subject further.

to another if entry to some of the niches in the industrial structure which they would be both happy and competent to fill is by one means or another blocked.

Opinion is naturally far from unanimous as to the extent to which it is either desirable or practicable to press the requirement of greater mobility. Some who are a little alarmed lest more mobility should be expected than they believe to be reasonable, seek to facilitate a solution of the problem as a whole by breaking it down into a number of parts, in some of which an attempt can be made to stabilize consumers' demand. Sir William Beveridge, for example, "emphasizes the need for stabilizing the demand for labour, not merely in total, but in each of its main categories."[1] He urges accordingly that "the outlay which is designed to produce full employment . . . must be directed to those industries and localities where idle labour and idle capacity can be brought together,"[2] and maintains that "deliberate direction of demand, with reference both to the industries and the places in which the workpeople can be found, will be an essential measure for prevention of unemployment."[3] It is partly for this purpose that control of the location of industry is frequently given a prominent place in programmes of full employment. More generally full employment policy has been described as "a policy of socializing demand,"[4] the organization of production to satisfy presumed "social" needs being carried a good deal further than in the now conventional fields of education, roads, hospitals, etc. The vigour with which these claims can be pressed depends in part on the extent to which consumers are prepared to sacrifice their right of individual choice in the interests of something else adjudged to have a higher "social priority". "A policy of socializing demand" might be carried so far as to limit very severely the freedom of the consumer to decide for himself what he would like to buy.

The risks of violent fluctuations in the demand for labour of particular kinds is naturally greatest in times like the present when, after a violent upheaval, a full recovery from whose effects is certain to be a lengthy and difficult business, our

---

[1] Beveridge, *Full Employment in a Free Society*, p. 269.
[2] Op. cit., p. 185.   [3] Op. cit., p. 169.   [4] Op. cit., p. 190.

economy has to deal with abnormally inflated demands, the satisfaction of which has had to be long delayed. The obvious illustration which at once comes to mind is housing. There is an urgent necessity for expansion in the construction of houses on an abnormal and unprecedented scale. It would be quite out of the question to defer so far to the interests of greater stability of employment in the building trades as to insist that this demand should be met at a pace much more deliberate than would conform to the convenience of those who now need houses. The immediate urgent demand must be met with the greatest possible speed. But if, again in the interests of stable employment, we were to prepare for a continuous programme of building over a further period, after urgent needs had been satisfied, there might be some risk that in a few years' time we should find ourselves pressing new houses upon consumers who would have preferred the community's resources to be mainly devoted to the provision of other things. And this is only one, though perhaps the most important, illustration of a dilemma which is always liable to present itself.

A special variant of the technique of diminishing the necessity for mobility by stabilizing employment in selected sectors of the economy rather than in the economy as a whole, which historically has been of the greatest importance, involves the free use of the instruments of commercial policy to control the entry of imports. This technique was extensively used during the inter-war period when to many it seemed obvious common sense to check or reverse a decline in the level of employment in home trades by excluding competitive foreign products. The repercussions of the widespread adoption of such plans, which in effect aimed at "exporting unemployment," were usually mutually frustrating, and for the most part it is now common ground among nearly all full employment theorists that, in future, such shortsighted devices for maintaining employment must be avoided. Some of the proposals held in reserve to meet the not improbable eventuality that general agreement on national full employment policies may not be possible have, however, a very close resemblance to some of the bad old practices of the depression of the thirties, and in view of the superficial attractiveness of such measures for those who do not look far ahead, it would be unduly optimistic to assume that we shall hear no more of them.

WAGE AND PRICE CONTROL

The control of prices and wages is perhaps not so much an integral part of a full employment programme, as a subordinate but very important safeguard, the absence of which, especially when the emphasis falls heavily upon fiscal measures, might threaten the disruption of an otherwise well-conceived plan. Most full employment programmes to-day contemplate at least a mild inflationary movement, and some would positively welcome movements as large as it was thought that the public would be prepared to tolerate, and in this background, some measures for keeping the movement of prices and of wages under control are inevitable. The White Paper, for example, postulated as the second of its "essential conditions" that "the level of prices and wages must be kept reasonably stable". The necessity for this condition arises in the following way. If the volume of purchasing power is maintained or expanded, either by public investment or by fiscal measures to support consumer expenditure or by a combination of these two techniques, there is always a risk either that the increments appropriate in any given circumstances may not be accurately estimated or that the available administrative devices may be ineffective in keeping the volume of purchasing power within proper limits. In either of these circumstances, the conditions will be favourable for an inflationary upward movement of prices, and this will be all the more likely if at an early stage the stream of purchasing power impinges with unusual force upon any of those sectors of the economy where for one reason or another supply reacts slowly to an increase in demand. These sectors will, in peace-time conditions, constitute bottlenecks of the same kind as those with which we have become familiar everywhere during the war. If, moreover, prices in these sectors are allowed to rise unduly, it will usually not be long before the movement is transmitted elsewhere, and a pressure for a corresponding wage adjustment is likely to be generated which itself would have further repercussions upon the price level. Full employment programmes therefore frequently include provision for the control of both prices and wages. Our judgment of the probable effectiveness of these controls must inevitably depend in part upon some considerations which are not exclusively economic. Most economies have during the war learnt a great deal about the technical side of price control, but we cannot count upon the favourable psychological conditions which have aided the task of the price-controller during war surviving to a sufficiently significant extent in peace. Nor would it be inconsistent to estimate the prospects of success quite differently in different economies. Even during the war the problems of price control have been quite different in India, for example, and in Great Britain, and these differences which arise from different social and economic backgrounds are not likely to disappear quickly after the war. This fact should be borne in mind in considering proposals for the transfer of the full employment techniques thought suitable in one country to other countries where different conditions may make them quite inapplicable.

More fundamental differences of opinion about the significance of this part of a full employment programme rest, however, upon a somewhat different foundation. Few would dispute the reality of the "bottleneck" problem, but there is much less agreement about its immediacy and its urgency, and disagreements on this issue are reflected in the difference of attitude between those who place most emphasis upon the fiscal approach to the whole problem of full employment, and in particular upon the maintenance of large government expenditures, and those who emphasize more the importance of the flexibility of the economic structure as a whole, and in particular the influence of the impediments placed in the way of expanding production in particular sectors of the economy. The first school do not deny the importance of "bottlenecks", but their proposals often imply that it is not particularly urgent to do anything about them at once. The members of the second school fear on the contrary that some "bottlenecks" will be encountered in the very earliest stages of full employment

programmes, and that if precautionary measures are postponed, many of the beneficial effects anticipated from the
application of the new techniques will quickly evaporate. If the
bottleneck problem is handled vigorously and without delay,
they believe, moreover, that the range within which the other
techniques will need to be applied, will be sensibly narrowed.
It might even be plausibly urged that the problem is already
with us, calling for immediate action. To a significant extent,
the problems of unemployment in the present arise from maldistributions of labour in the past. If we ignore the checks and
limitations which have produced and continue to produce these
maldistributions, we shall be constantly confronted in the
future with similar problems. Instead of waiting to deal piecemeal with the subsequent effects of these maldistributions as
they arise, it would be better, it is argued, to take steps now to
correct some at least of their fundamental causes.

The significance for international economic policy of the
elements of policy thus briefly outlined, is far from uniform.
Some of the methods of maintaining full employment will
create difficulties for other countries; others will not, and it
will be part of the purpose of our subsequent analysis to show
how far the acuteness of international problems might be
mitigated or intensified by varying the emphasis placed upon
the various techniques which we have listed.

Chapter IV

THE CONCEPT OF AN OPEN INTERNATIONAL
ECONOMIC ORDER (1)

FULL employment and an open international system are both objectives to which, in somewhat different ways, Great Britain is now formally committed. But while full employment is widely accepted as an end desirable in itself, even the warmest supporters of an open international system do not think of it as more than a means for the attainment of other ends, though in so far as they regard it as a certain and perhaps even the only means to ends so highly approved by them, they sometimes come very near to identifying ends with means. On the other hand, some of the critics of an open international order, in their eagerness to discredit the means which are assumed to be an essential part of such an order, have sometimes also cast doubt upon the value of the ends whose attainment is its ultimate purpose.

An analysis of the meaning and implications of full employment is, therefore, naturally followed in the present study by a similar analysis of the concept of an open international order, and the very fact that, especially in Great Britain, the social forces lying behind the drive towards full employment are obviously stronger than any upon which the movement to re-establish an open international system is based, justifies us in taking special care over this part of our argument.

The two analyses cannot, indeed, proceed along exactly parallel lines, for there are several significant differences between the methods likely to be most effective for eliciting the essential meaning of the two objectives. Whether or not full employment has ever in the past been maintained over any period of time is a question whose answer will naturally depend upon our definition of the term. It is frequently claimed that full employment was attained during the inter-war period in both the U.S.S.R. and Germany, but the conditions of its realization in each of these economies are matters still hotly disputed, and probably included some important elements which most exponents of full employment in other countries would now insist must be avoided. Apart from these debatable exceptions, it can be plausibly represented that no historical illustrations of full employment, at least of a kind significant for the purposes of British policy, can be discovered, so that except by way of contrast with the past, an analysis of full employment need not concern itself much with history. Full employment is to-day the object of many careful and elaborate detailed plans, and if we wish to discover the true inwardness of full employment, we shall probably find it more profitable to analyse and probe behind these plans than to spend much time in historical study. It is, however, doubtful whether at any time anyone has sat down to work out a blue-print for a standard liberal international economic order. Its underlying doctrinal foundations have seldom been clearly enunciated in full, and much less fully realized in practice. There has, however, been one important period in world history when the policies of the more important economies were determined more or less closely according to its principles, and during which its institutional forms were undergoing a process of continuous evolution. For many purposes, therefore, the most convenient method for elucidating the meaning of an open international economic order is by way of an historical analysis of the experience of this period.

THE NINETEENTH CENTURY SYSTEM

Current discussions of international trade policy are frequently prefaced by an analysis of the "implicit assumptions" which, it is claimed, formed the basis of the classical theory of international trade. But even if this analysis is not open to criticism in detail, its general effects are misleading if it suggests, as it often appears to do, that at some time during the nineteenth century somebody worked out an abstract theory of international trade, which was then accepted as the justification for the practical details of the "open" international system subsequently put into operation. The interaction of theory and practice is always an intricate business, and the influence of theoretical analysis upon the evolution of commercial policy in Great Britain was not negligible. But for the most part the system of the nineteenth and early twentieth centuries was maintained and developed, not on account of any doctrinaire respect for theory, but because it was widely, though not indeed universally, accepted as meeting certain fundamental requirements to which most people at the time attached great importance. The institutions and policies which, in retrospect, we now identify as characteristic of such an order were gradually evolved over a long period of time, and under the impact of current problems of varying content and varying degrees of relative urgency. It is a matter of no little difficulty to determine precisely the limits of the period which most fully exemplifies the practical operations of the open international system, and the same reasons which explain this fluidity also justify the expectation that any post-war "open" system which we may succeed in constructing will differ in many significant respects from anything which has preceded it. It may also be safely predicted that, like its predecessor, it too will present a difficult problem to those who insist on clear-cut and precise definitions and classifications. It will include many anomalies and even contradictions, and those responsible for its inauguration will have to be prepared for a continuous process of adjustment and compromise. At certain periods of the nineteenth century an observer might have felt that Adam Smith had been over-cautious when he declared that "to expect that freedom of trade should ever be entirely restored in Great Britain is as absurd as to expect that an Oceana or Utopia should ever be established in it", but we should certainly be wise to temper in a no less cautious spirit any expectations we may cherish about any new international economic system which we may hope to establish.

Alongside the development of practice there was a more or less parallel development of theory in which, for purposes of precision, it was found convenient to make certain assumptions; assumptions, for example, concerning the mobility of factors of production within national economies, and their immobility between national economies. But critics of the old international order have often exaggerated the practical significance of these assumptions, and whatever defects there may have been in the "classical" theory of international trade have little relevance to the current necessity or desirability of changes in international economic policy or practice. In some minds, such changes are inexorably imposed by the new situation which the irreversible course of recent events has created, and a rational justification for the change is sought, either in the fact that the ends which an open system helped to achieve are now thought to be less important than other ends which have come to be highly regarded, or in significant changes which are alleged to have occurred in the concrete conditions of production to which the structure of international exchange has to be adapted.

It might with very little exaggeration be claimed that the essential characteristic of the "open" international order which evolved during the nineteenth century was just the simple fact that it was international. International trade had, of course, already had a long and chequered history, and the nineteenth century is not clearly separated from the periods which preceded it by any point of time at which it can be said that the content and status of international trade were then definitely transformed. Nevertheless, there is a recognizable contrast between the earlier centuries, dominated by national economies, when the processes of production, exchange and consumption were normally completed within the boundaries of a nation, and the new conditions in which a more or less deliberate effort was made to extend the range of economic relations beyond these limits. Statistical measurements of the volume of international trade give only an inadequate picture of the significant trends, for changes in the character and content of trade, which more and more made many economies increasingly dependent for some of the elements essential for their everyday life upon the maintenance of regular connections with the outside world, were often more important than any change in the volume of trade as a whole. The degree of dependence was naturally not uniform. It was unusually great for Great Britain, and perhaps partly for this reason there was a keener consciousness in Great Britain than in some other countries of the significance of the trend of events, though to a lesser degree other countries, too, were moving in the same direction.

Already by the beginning of the nineteenth century it was coming to be more and more generally accepted that, within national economies, the most satisfactory results would be forthcoming if resources of labour and capital were allowed to distribute themselves in such a way as to equalize their marginal products in all parts of the economy. The urge to establish an international order was motivated by the belief that similar satisfactory results would follow if similar principles were allowed to operate in determining the allocation of industries as between different countries. Many exceptions to this principle were admitted. Economic theory has always paid a good deal of attention to the importance of divergences between private net marginal product and social net marginal product, and it has always been possible that these divergences might justify the establishment of certain industries in countries other than those marked out as suitable by a strict comparison of costs. Whether the practical importance of this possibility was likely to be great in any given instance depended upon an examination of the facts of the case, and the efforts made to obstruct the adjustments necessary if net marginal products were to be equalized were often motivated by considerations of quite a different kind.

The equalization of net marginal products within a national economy presupposed a high degree of mobility within it of the various factors of production. As between one country and another this condition was often realized only very imperfectly, and a theory of international trade was developed to show that, where factors of production were immobile, it would pay each country to specialize in the production of those commodities in relation to which it enjoyed the greatest comparative advantage. Theoretically several methods might have been conceived for the measurement of comparative costs, but as a direct comparison would often be difficult unless competing goods were brought into the market and there submitted to the final test of purchasers' preferences, and as the pressure of competition from abroad was the only reliable agency for shaping an economy towards the most generally profitable pattern of specialization, it was widely taken for granted that the organization of international trade on this basis demanded a reasonable degree of freedom in competition between the traders of different countries. A little paradoxically, in view of the important part assigned in the theory of international trade to the hypothesis of immobility, the practical benefits accruing from the development of an "open" international system in the nineteenth century were to no small extent tied up with the unusual degree of freedom to move from one economy to another enjoyed at that time by both labour and capital. Impediments to free movement were widely felt to be inconsistent with the basic principles of the "open" system, whose purpose it was in effect to reproduce, so far as was possible in the economic relations between different countries, conditions similar to those which are normal in the relations of regions inside a country.

These points can be put in another way by saying that among the ends which ranked highest in the minds of supporters of an open international order, was the creation and maintenance of a condition in which producers in each country could compete with producers in all other countries upon terms which ensured that, subject to limited and defined exceptions, the low-cost producer would get the business. This condition was to a considerable extent realized during the nineteenth century. In recent years the exceptions have been widely extended, and their limits are no longer easily defined. Any serious effort to establish an open system on a new basis would seek to reverse this trend.

THE MOST FAVOURED NATION PRINCIPLE

The doctrine of preference to low-cost producers found formal expression in the two principles of "national treatment" and "most favoured nation treatment", which, in varying forms of words, are now embodied in a vast and intricate network of international treaties. The principle of "national treatment" guarantees to the citizens of any one of the parties to a treaty the same treatment as the citizens of the other receive in relation to the matters specified in the treaty. Whether

46

the admission of this principle will, in practice, ensure the absence of discrimination, will inevitably depend on a large number of considerations, administrative and otherwise, and there are some matters, e.g. in relation to the ownership of land, to coastal shipping and fisheries, etc., where "national treatment," in the sense defined, is by no means universally practised. This principle has, however, on the whole, provoked less criticism than the principle of "most favoured nation treatment", according to which (in its unconditional form) each of the contracting parties agrees to accord to goods imported from the other tariff treatment no less favourable than that given to goods imported from any third country, with exceptions commonly admitted for colonies, contiguous states, and states with which customs unions are in force. In the nineteenth and early twentieth centuries, great importance was attached to the most favoured nation principle, as it was believed that in the course of time its application would make possible a gradual reduction everywhere of barriers to trade. During certain periods in the nineteenth century, there was indeed good reason for taking seriously the expectation that from time to time tariffs and other obstacles to trade would be modified as a result of direct negotiations between pairs of countries, and that these modifications would then have to be automatically extended to third parties.

CONSUMERS AND PRODUCERS

No less important in the ideology implicit in the practice of an open international system than the respect paid to the interests of low-cost producers, was the principle of the supremacy of consumers' wants. It was regarded as axiomatic that, in the last resort, no one was more competent than the final consumer himself to decide what was to be produced and where it was to be produced. Left to himself, the final consumer will, no doubt, make many mistakes, but the risks of error on his part were believed to be very much less than the risks of error on the part of any other authority which might assume responsibility for these decisions.

The freedom of consumers will be seriously limited, unless

people in each country can freely spend in any country they may choose the proceeds of their sales in any other country. Unless, therefore, conditions permit the development of international trade on multilateral lines, without any reference to the balances of payments between selected pairs or groups of countries, there can be no open international system. Multilateralism is equally essential if the rights of low-cost producers are to be respected, for otherwise specialization will be unable to develop in accordance with the most generally advantageous geographical pattern. From either standpoint, any deviations from multilateralism before 1914 were of little importance.

The conditions which determine who are the low-cost producers are sure to alter from time to time; the efficient administration of an open system therefore demands a high degree of flexibility within the national economies participating in it, a sufficient degree of willingness to allow some sectors of industry to contract while others expand. Continuous enjoyment of the benefits to be derived from international division of labour demands that there should be no undue sluggishness on the part of the resources of production, capital and labour, in responding to changes in the comparative cost situation and transferring to new fields of investment and employment. However inconvenient this might be to some producers, it was widely felt in the nineteenth century to be generally fair to producers as a whole. The market allocations registered at any moment of time in the trade statistics of the world are the result of a series of historical accidents, to which no particular sanctity can be attributed, and it would be unfair to crystallize these allocations by refusing to producers who had improved their standards of efficiency the opportunity to supply goods and services which, in the new conditions which are constantly arising, potential foreign customers would be glad to have. And if adjustments of market conditions are to be allowed from time to time, it would be equally unfair to base the new allocations on anything but the relative efficiency of rival producers. However radical the changes which we may contemplate in the institutional structure of the post-war international economic system, serious discussion of the restoration of an "open" order is scarcely possible

48

unless a high priority is granted to the serious application of this principle. The participants in an open order must be prepared to face the necessity for structural adjustments within their own national economies, and to realize, moreover, that inasmuch as the processes of adjustment must be continuous, this problem can never be finally "solved".

THE LONDON MONEY MARKET

The machinery of the world monetary system, without which no world trading system could have evolved on the lines here indicated, was highly flexible, with an almost complete absence of formal obligation imposed upon those who participated in it. In practice the part played by sterling in this system was so important that it might almost seem a matter of indifference whether the nineteenth century economic order was described as a British or an international order. There was one dominating centre which in respect of many important matters could usually, largely because its leadership was normally beneficent, count on being able to give an effective lead and to get its own way. The gold standard of this period was, to all intents and purposes, a sterling standard; the efficiency of the operations of the world's monetary system was such that for the most part it was simply taken for granted, and there is still no universal doctrine to explain the precise manner of its working. This condition may have been natural and healthy enough at the time; it had, however, the unfortunate consequence that even "experts" often had little understanding of the underlying principles, tending to think mainly in terms of technicalities, the precise form of which was sometimes a matter almost of accident, and it was this state of mind which after 1918, when the normal background had been violently disrupted, encouraged an undue pre-occupation with pre-war exchange rates which by that time had ceased to have much more than an historical interest. Each currency was convertible into any other currency, and usually at a fixed and invariable rate, though especially among some of the less important economies there were a good many exceptions to this rule. For the most important economies, however, that free convertibility of currencies which made multilateralism possible came to be so highly regarded that a characteristic, which strictly speaking might have been described as merely part of the technical apparatus of an "open" system, came to be thought of as constituting its real essence. And the existence of unstable currencies during the nineteenth century, with effects of some importance upon international trade, is of less interest than the fact that probably at no time did it occur to those responsible for national policy that a fluctuating exchange rate could be made a deliberate objective, or that a foreign exchange position could be used as a bargaining factor to secure a larger share of either world trade or world production.

The narrowly monetary side of the machinery thus centred in London was perhaps less important than the credit and investment operations inextricably linked with it. In retrospect, indeed, we may too readily overlook some of the problems associated with the international flow of capital which at the time caused considerable concern. Looking at the nineteenth century as a whole, we may say that the bulk of the world's foreign lending was undertaken by investors of long experience and reasonable caution, and was accordingly directed to development which paid fairly well. But the qualities of mind and character needed for effective leadership in this field were not simply the free gifts of nature. Experience had to be acquired, and especially in the first half of the century there was a good deal of rash foreign investment which on a more modest scale foreshadowed some of the disasters of the inter-war period. Difficulties also sometimes arose from abrupt interruptions in the flow of capital, though there was nothing comparable with the sudden cessation of United States foreign lending after 1929, and broadly speaking the readjustments which from time to time became necessary were carried through without much serious risk of disturbance to national balances of payments of the kind which in recent years have become an almost universal preoccupation. In this the relatively free movements of capital, both long-term and short-term, which were a characteristic feature of the system, played an important part, usually providing a sufficient margin for necessary adjustments to be carried through without undue strain.

The extent and far-sightedness of London's control can indeed easily be exaggerated. While the influence of British policy and example was always substantial, it was far from sufficient to establish a world system which conformed in every respect to the theoretical principles of a liberal order. And even in the fields where British influence was most direct and most effective, it was often much less consciously exercised than one might gather from some of the subsequent attempts to paint a consistent picture of the working of the system as a whole. It is indeed a curious fact that despite the generally admitted importance of British "leadership" during this period, there is still no general agreement either about the way in which it actually worked or about the limits, self-imposed or otherwise, to its influence.[1]

MOBILITY OF LABOUR AND CAPITAL

The historical decline of the liberal international order proceeded *pari passu* with the growth of restrictions upon the

---

[1] The picture of the nineteenth century system presented by Professor Carr, who describes it as "at once supra-national and British" rather than international, is certainly overdrawn. "The Bank of England", he says, "as custodian of the integrity of sterling, found itself—unwillingly, and for the most part unwittingly—the final arbiter and court of appeal and the central executive authority of the international system of trade and finance. All gold-standard countries had to keep pace with one another in expanding and contracting the flow of money and trade; and it was the London market which inevitably set the pace. Just as mercantilism in the seventeenth and eighteenth centuries had transformed local economies into a single national economy, so in the nineteenth century, the merchants, brokers and bankers of London, acting under the sovereign responsibility of the 'old lady of Threadneedle Street', transformed the national economies into a single world economy." (*Nationalism and After*, London, Macmillan, 1945, pp. 14-16.) Professor Viner, on the other hand, declares that Sir John Clapham's *The Bank of England* (Cambridge University Press, 1944), "reveals little or nothing to confirm the belief that the Bank, or any other English institution, deliberately or otherwise 'managed' the gold standard . . . . To the extent that sterling balances were serviceable abroad as monetary reserves, London, by granting credit abroad more freely in times of strain and contracting it in times of dangerous expansion, could have exercised a stabilizing role *vis-à-vis* the international gold standard . . . . But I know of no evidence that London played such a role, and as far as available information goes, it may even be possible that London typically reduced her credits to abroad when it was most urgent that she should expand them and expanded them when contraction would have been more beneficial. It seems clear that as far as long-term loans were concerned, England accentuated the cyclical fluctuations in the level of world activity rather than damped them down, and this for all we know may have been true also of her short-term transactions." (*Economica*, May, 1945, pp. 63-4.)

freedom of migration and of international capital movements, and this fact obliges us to raise the further question, how far the requirement of flexibility also necessitates the maintenance of such a high degree of international mobility of labour and capital as was frequently permitted during the nineteenth and early twentieth centuries. This is no doubt one of the numerous questions concerning which the truth is a matter of degree. No one who desired the reconstruction of an "open" system would be lukewarm in support of any movement which had a reasonable chance of success, for the revival either of international investment or of freer migration. It is not merely the peculiar difficulties of the immediate transitional period into which we are now entering which justify the view that without large-scale international capital movements the prospects for the re-building of some tolerable kind of world order will be very poor. International investment in one form or another is an important item in nearly all reconstruction programmes, and for many areas talk about expanding production of the types demanded by the comparative cost principle would have little meaning unless there were a considerable influx of capital from outside. Whether precisely the same degree of freedom is now necessary as prevailed during a large part of the nineteenth century is, however, a much more debatable proposition. In particular the forces which limit freedom of migration are still very powerful, and practical men may hesitate to spend much time in discussing hypothetical movements of population which are quite unlikely to occur.

Even if large-scale migration had been an absolutely essential condition of the nineteenth century system, it would not necessarily follow that it had the same degree of importance for a new "open" system under the changed conditions in which we are now living. The basic economic condition lying behind the large-scale migrations which came to an end just before 1914 was the urgent need of the world as a whole for increased supplies of certain products whose output could not easily be rapidly expanded without large increases of population in the most important countries of immigration. The world still has large unsatisfied urgent needs, but their character has changed, and the increased output which it is now most important to organize could without great difficulty be made available without large-scale shifts of population. The current technological trends, which, as we shall see later, many have thought were diminishing the benefits to be derived from international specialization, and therefore weakening the case for the maintenance of an open international system, may indeed rather have had the opposite effect of making it easier to restore such a system, even though the condition of comparatively free migration with which it had been intimately associated during the nineteenth century was no longer likely to be fulfilled.

THE OPEN SYSTEM IN THEORY AND PRACTICE

The allocation of industries, and therefore of world trade, between different national economies has never been determined exclusively by reference to the considerations which we have been discussing. National tariffs have always been a modifying factor of the utmost importance, and especially in recent years vigorous efforts have been made to direct world trade into channels different from those indicated by a comparison of relative costs and efficiencies. Nevertheless, the influence of the ideas lying behind the theory of an "open" system was throughout the nineteenth and early twentieth centuries both extensive and profound. Radical adjustments were imposed upon many national economies, and, on the whole, with great advantage to their productive efficiency and to the standards of living enjoyed by their inhabitants. The evolution of the open system was itself in part an expression of a climate of opinion which was becoming more and more favourable to bold departures from established ways, and in turn it helped to create an atmosphere highly favourable for pioneers. It can scarcely be an accident that it was during the period when the ideas upon which the open international system was based played an important if not a dominant role, that the world as a whole entered upon a period of unprecedentedly rapid expansion without parallel at any other stage of world history. It is true that the benefits were not equally shared. To many it appeared that Great Britain was the outstanding beneficiary, and British devotion to the principles of the system was no doubt based primarily upon a sound judgment of current British interests. The old free-trade doctrine, it has been said, was "merely a device for continuing British industrial supremacy. Free Trade was good business for England, and also it was good business for her to have every one else do likewise."[1] Too many of the modern English writers who are hostile to traditional nineteenth century policy have, however, been imprudently eager to defer to this prejudiced view of British policy. There is no justification for the belief, which they tend to encourage, that Britain's gains were in general or indeed in any intelligible sense of the words made "at the expense" of other people, or that British policy at that time did not also imply substantial benefits for many and perhaps for most other economies. It was not only Great Britain which forged rapidly ahead during the period when the basic principles of an open international system exercised their greatest influence. Other economies too improved their position, and to such an extent that if a table could be constructed showing the countries of the world graded according to their *per capita* income or their general prosperity the picture thus presented for 1914 would reveal many striking changes as compared with the picture of fifty years or a century earlier. These changes could not have occurred without a large measure of adjustment in the structure of production of the national economies concerned of the kind which we have seen is essential for the smooth working of an open international order. We should not underrate the severity of the strains which these adjustments imposed, though few economies during this period were actually called upon to submit to the severe deflationary pressures which subsequently were made almost the chief ground of attack upon the rigidities believed to be inevitable in an international monetary system. But whatever may subsequently have been thought of the incidental inconveniences arising from their close integration with the more advanced economies of the West, many of the overseas regions whose standards of living are now among the highest in the world would under any other system only

[1] Samuel Crowther, *America Self-Contained*, New York, Doubleday-Doran, 1933, p. 177.

with the utmost difficulty have made the rapid strides which marked their economic growth during this period, and the contrast between widespread poverty at the beginning of the nineteenth century and comparative affluence at its conclusion is no less striking in some of the smaller European economies than in Great Britain herself.

There is no invisible hand which inevitably ensures harmony between the interests of different national economies, but equally there is no justification for the opposite view that there is or ever was any inevitable conflict between British interests and the interests of other countries. It is now a legitimate matter for debate whether a reconstructed open system would be beneficial either to Great Britain or to the rest of the world, but the real benefits associated with membership of the nineteenth century system should not be discounted by implying that they were exclusively or mainly British. Nor is the hypothesis of the generally beneficial character of the nineteenth century system seriously weakened by the fact that many economies found it convenient from time to time to depart from its strict principles. For in many cases the advantages which by this means they hoped to enjoy were contingent upon their confident expectation, usually justified by the event, that Great Britain would not follow their example. "One may talk cynically about the motives of the English during the nineteenth century; but", as an American writer has recently said, "one may not now question the good results of English hegemony in terms of peace and progress."[1]

---

[1] Henry C. Simons, "Trade and the Peace", in *Post-War Economic Problems*, ed. Seymour E. Harris, New York, McGraw Hill, 1943, p. 145.

Chapter V

THE CONCEPT OF AN OPEN INTERNATIONAL ECONOMIC ORDER (2)

THE EXPERIENCE OF THE INTER-WAR PERIOD

EVEN before 1914 the picture which we have just outlined was never fully realized. During the inter-war period it became fashionable to say that the old order had "broken down". Machinery which has "broken down" usually stops working altogether, and when one recalls that the majority of international trade transactions were still carried on in accordance with the old principles and by the old methods, it may be felt that the pessimistic view implied in the use of this phrase was exaggerated. The departures from the principles of an open system were, however, numerous and far-reaching, and their fundamental value was more and more called in question. It would be scarcely an exaggeration to say that in many economies the protection of high-cost producers became the dominant factor in economic policy, while in the technique of trade finance the contrast with the conditions of the earlier period is most clearly visible in terms of the widespread adoption and approval of bilateralist practices, the administration of which often demanded a severe disciplining of the free expression of consumers' desires.

The prestige which the most favoured nation principle had formerly enjoyed also began to decline. The knowledge that any modification of trade restrictions conceded in a commercial treaty had to be extended to third parties was often a sufficient reason to ensure that no far-reaching modifications were made, and treaty rights were invoked, as in the case of the Ouchy Convention of 1932, to prevent the implementation of limited reductions of trade barriers which infringed the most favoured nation privileges of other states. Many in Great Britain who favoured the ideas lying behind the once fashionable phrase, a "low-tariff club", denounced the most favoured nation principle as a dangerous obstacle to that piecemeal approach to the relaxation of trade restrictions which, in the unprecedented complexities of the modern world, seemed to them the only practical method for reversing the restrictionist trend.

Every one knows that tariffs of the old-fashioned type have in recent years played a role of steadily diminishing importance in the commercial policies of many economies, and the serious difficulties created by attempts to adapt the most favoured nation principle to the quota regulations and exchange controls which have replaced them have been widely taken as a further justification for the belief that this principle no longer has much relevance in modern conditions. This problem presented itself in the most acute form to the United States officials charged with the responsibility of putting into effect the Reciprocal Trade Act, passed first in 1934 and subsequently renewed on several occasions. For it has been their task to ensure that no agreements should be made with countries guilty of "discriminatory treatment of American commerce." A doctrinaire interpretation of this responsibility would probably have reduced the number of agreements to an insignificant figure, for it could easily have been argued that quota regulations and foreign exchange controls were from their very nature discriminatory, and the number of countries which to a greater or less extent had resorted to these practices was so great that on an austere interpretation of discrimination the list of potential treaty-partners for the United States would necessarily be very short. It is theoretically conceivable that quota regulations might be made sufficiently flexible to take due account of changes in the competitive efficiency of rival suppliers, but even in theory this is scarcely conceivable for exchange controls, and the chances that theoretical possibilities would in any way be reflected in the practical administration of quota regulations cannot in any event be rated very high. In practice the difficulties were often provisionally overcome by a compromise whose results did not appear at the time to conflict too seriously with the objective of United States policy. But at best these compromises merely ensured that trade positions built up in an arbitrarily selected historical period should be preserved, a solution which necessarily failed to ensure that flexibility which is an essential condition for an effective "open" international system. The compromises with which United States negotiators had to be satisfied for the time being could not be regarded as anything more than a temporary solution, and opinion in the United States, which regarded the reconstruction of an open system as an objective of first-rate importance, both politically and economically, took it as axiomatic that this implied the restoration of the free convertibility of national currencies and the progressive abandonment of exchange control.

To the tension and confusion of the inter-war period many economies made their significant contributions, but the potential strength and widespread influence of the United States gave a peculiar importance to the policy of that country. Something will be said later about the widespread criticisms of the alleged chronic instability of the United States economy, but, more directly in the field of commercial relations, the difficult situation of many economies was rendered still more difficult by United States crisis decisions. It is natural that our appreciation of the wisdom of flexibility in economic structure should normally be keener when it is a question of other people adjusting themselves to changed conditions than when we are asked to do the same thing ourselves, and though flexibility has always been an outstanding characteristic of many sectors of the United States economy, in that country, as elsewhere, there has also always been much strong and successful resistance to the full application of the doctrine of preference to low-cost producers. The traditional reluctance to allow the "sacrifice" of home producers to foreign competition was strongly reinforced during the depression years, especially in relation to the farming population, even before doctrines of full employment began to suggest that there was a case for "stabilizing the demand for labour in each of its main categories". The extent to which United States opinion will permit a radical modification of policies based upon this attitude will be one of the most important factors determining the future shape of international economic relations.

STERLING IN THE SECOND WORLD WAR

Even in 1939 the architects of a new open international order would therefore have had to face a world situation where their freedom of manoeuvre was gravely limited in many directions, and the financial consequences of the war have further changed the situation with which we have to deal, introducing many new and intractable features which the practical statesman cannot ignore. Great Britain is not the only economy directly affected by these changes, but as they certainly affect Great Britain at least as profoundly—and in certain respects indeed more so— as any other economy, and our interest here is the reconciliation of possible divergent obligations for British policy, it will be sufficient for us to examine the British position as it has been affected by the war.

Until 1939 sterling was one of the world currencies, holders of which, wherever they might happen to be, could confidently count on being able at their own discretion to dispose of their holdings without any fear of restriction. A sterling bloc had developed which embraced a number of countries with close trading relations with Great Britain and who on that account found it convenient to hold a considerable fraction of their currency reserves in London in the form of sterling balances. They could, however, always deal with these holdings as they themselves thought fit. Sterling balances were a convenient form of currency reserve just because they could at any time without any difficulty be converted into any other currency which might be needed. As it developed, the machinery of the sterling bloc provided substantial benefits for its members, but without imposing any disability or inconvenience upon other economies outside its boundaries.

During the war it was out of the question that this convenient convertibility of sterling could be maintained. The requirements of foreign currency, and particularly of dollars, necessary to finance the purchase of supplies essential for the war effort, were so pressing that not only was it necessary to control and ultimately to destroy the freedom of holders of sterling to use it to purchase foreign currencies to be spent for purposes of their

own, but overseas assets in British ownership were also com-
mandeered and liquidated in order to increase the supply of
foreign currencies available for essential military purposes. In
these circumstances, the character of the pre-war sterling bloc
has inevitably been completely transformed, so much so indeed
as to raise doubts whether it is legitimate to use the same term
to describe the new machinery which has for the time being
taken its place. For the most part the non-Commonwealth
members of the bloc ceased to participate in it, and it became an
essential feature of the bloc that holders of sterling were no
longer free to do as they pleased with their holdings except
within the sterling area itself, while the limited supplies of
foreign currencies available for this bloc as a whole were rationed
in accordance with the varying requirements of the changing
war situation. Some members of the new sterling bloc sold large
quantities of supplies to Great Britain for which payment was
accepted in sterling subject to these limitations, and the volume
of these sterling balances, often popularly though a little mis-
leadingly described as "blocked", is now very great. The total
sterling liabilities to overseas countries were estimated to exceed
£3,355 millions on June 30, 1945,[1] India being the largest
single holder, and though this figure may give an exaggerated
impression of the claims which the holders of balances would
wish to make good immediately, the situation which they create
is clearly one of abnormal difficulty. The balances thus accumulated are not, strictly speaking, "blocked", as they are usually
available to finance purchases made in other parts of the sterling
area outside Great Britain. Limitations of supply and shortages
of transport, however, considerably limit the practical significance of these formal rights, and to all intents and purposes the
larger part of the balances represent claims upon British export
production which for the time being their holders have been content not to press, but which at a later date they hope to make

[1] Cmd. 6707. Of this total £2,723 millions was due to countries within the
sterling area, with a balance of £632 millions which had accumulated to the
credit of countries outside. The geographical limits of the sterling area have
fluctuated a little from time to time during the war. At the beginning of
1946 it included the British Empire, with the exception of Canada and
Newfoundland, Egypt, the Anglo-Egyptian Sudan, Iraq, Iceland, and
the Faroe Islands.

good. They are in effect loans to Great Britain for an undefined period of time the manner of whose ultimate liquidation is still somewhat uncertain.

It seems, however, highly improbable that, if reliance is placed exclusively upon current British production, these claims can be liquidated at a rate satisfactory to all their holders, eager as they naturally are to develop the productive capacity of their own economies, which in varying degrees have also been upset by the war. The manner of their liquidation in such circumstances might not be easily reconcilable with the expeditious recon-struction of a normal open international system, and on this account as well as for other reasons, suggestions have been put forward for either an orderly scaling down of these obligations, or for some kind of supplementary special arrangement to ensure that holders of sterling will without undue delay be able to satisfy at least a part of their requirements. Both these sug-gestions find a place in Article 10 of the Financial Agreement of December 1945, which registers the intention of the Govern-ment of the United Kingdom to make agreements with the countries concerned for an early settlement of these accumulated balances, one of the categories into which the balances are to fall being described as "balances to be adjusted as a contribu-tion to the settlement of war and post-war indebtedness and in recognition of the benefits which the countries concerned might be expected to gain from such a settlement." The arrangements, however, have still to be made, and though the principle is no doubt also approved by the Government of the United States, it may be no easy task to reconcile the views of all the Govern-ments directly concerned.

The restrictions imposed by membership of the war-time sterling bloc have been readily accepted as a war-time necessity. There were indeed obvious advantages to be gained from pool-ing foreign exchange resources, for most of the economies concerned were in much the same position as Great Britain herself. The new circumstances, however, inevitably make ster-ling less attractive to overseas exporters. Before the war they accepted it without question because they knew that at any time they liked they could convert it into some other currency and buy whatever they liked in any part of the world. This right no longer exists, and the limitations imposed upon the convertibility of sterling naturally therefore carry with them a tendency towards similar limitations upon its acceptability. In the meantime, as the cessation of hostilities has made possible the resumption of limited trade with liberated and neutral European countries as well as with other parts of the world, provisional *ad hoc* arrangements have had to be made for financing these exchanges. From the British standpoint the most convenient immediate solution is an arrangement whereby purchasers on either side can build up liabilities on the basis of the mutual provision of overdraft facilities, with or without a defined limit, which ensure that trade shall not be impeded by shortages of currency in either direction. In view of the current supply situation, some of these countries are likely to be able to meet some of Great Britain's needs more promptly than they can get their own requirements satisfied in Great Britain, so that the arrangements made along these lines are likely to result in a further accumulation of sterling balances the use of which is limited in the way already described. Willingness to allow such arrangements to run on indefinitely will naturally diminish as war-time crisis conditions tend to disappear. Countries which export to Great Britain have an understandable prejudice in favour of being paid for their exports without undue delay.

It seldom happens in human affairs that we are presented with a clean sheet upon which we can draw any picture which happens to please us. At any given moment we must start from the facts as they have developed up to that time, and though the facts seldom prescribe a single direction for policy to which no alternative of any kind is even conceivable, they limit the range within which it is profitable to spend time discussing alternative possibilities. The view is sometimes held that the trend which we have just described foreshadows the direction in which British commercial policy must now inevitably move. It is not the thesis of the present study that we are so helplessly entangled in the web of history; nevertheless, any realistic discussion of the possibility of restoring a new international open order must include these facts, as they have developed during the war and are still developing at the present time, as part of the background within which policy has now to be worked out.

THE BRITISH AND THE AMERICAN POST-WAR PROBLEMS

These circumstances to a large extent explain the current differences in the tone in which post-war policy is now being discussed in Great Britain and in the United States. Inevitably the pressure is not felt in precisely the same place, and in contemplating a restored open system, the aspect of the problem which attracts most interest and receives most emphasis is naturally not the same in the two countries. There is nothing in the economic situation of the United States to give the people of that country any direct experience of the fears upon which British sensitiveness to the risks of a disordered balance of payments is based. For the United States in fact there is no exchange problem; for the United Kingdom, on the contrary, this is necessarily Problem No. 1. When Americans express a resolute determination either to restore an old international system or to establish a new system on reformed lines, the motive most powerful in their minds is often the desire to have as wide outlets as possible for their own low-cost producers. Many of the negatives implicit in the principles of an open system find their most forcible expression to-day, and especially in the United States, in the grand assault on "discrimination", which has been formally authorized by the Article of the Mutual Aid Agreement already quoted, and the defence of the principle of preference to low-cost producers is among the most influential motives lying behind this drive. Cynics have indeed been free with the suggestion that in the United States there is a much more lively interest in taking quick advantage of temporary competitive superiorities than in the establishment of any stable international order strictly so called. It would, however, be evidence of a deplorable spirit of defeatism to allow it to be understood that in the long run preference to low-cost producers was not regarded as also an important British interest, and we should perhaps be wise to hesitate in pressing these criticisms too far, for they readily provoke the embarrassing counter-charge that we lack confidence in our own capacity to establish a sound competitive position for ourselves, and for that reason have decided to try to develop our international trade on foundations other than the merits of the goods and services we want to sell.

Discrimination should perhaps be added to the long list of important concepts for which no precise or exact definition can easily be found, and it is an attractive, though usually also an unprofitable, activity to pillory the inconsistency of some of those most ardent in their denunciation of the discriminatory practices of others. It would, however, be a mistake to press these difficulties so far as to imply that we in Great Britain were not sensible of the risks we would run if the world were encouraged to regard discrimination, however defined, as respectable. Any attempt at an exhaustive codification of discriminatory practices would no doubt reveal many borderline cases in the interpretation of which the critics might in perfect good faith disagree. But most of those which have much practical importance are not difficult to recognize, and remembering that discrimination might easily be directed against ourselves with highly embarrassing consequences, we should hesitate to elaborate the sophisms which suggest that discrimination has no meaning at all.

The practical significance of the most favoured nation principle has undoubtedly diminished in recent years. Nevertheless, it may be questioned whether any willingness on our part to take the initiative in establishing a world where national commercial policies were entirely free from the formal restraints imposed by traditional adherence to the principle might not turn out to be an unhappy illustration of the human weakness which too often assumes that, if we change our habits to suit our convenience, other people and other nations will continue to behave just as they did in the past. We now know a good deal about the consequences, both for ourselves and for the rest of the world, of a decision by one powerful economy to mould its policy without any reference to the philosophy lying behind the most favoured nation principle. But we have no experience at all of the probable consequences of a number of such decisions taken simultaneously by a large number of economies, and we might prudently take some time to examine the consequences before making any decision of this kind for ourselves. At least we should not too hastily set aside as unworthy of serious consideration the possibility that the obstructions which have so restricted the effectiveness of the most favoured nation principle might not be removed by other kinds of collaborative action, so that the risks of economic warfare implicit in proposals for scrapping it might be avoided.

It is useful from time to time to remind the people and politicians of Great Britain of the long-run importance of these considerations. Nevertheless, in existing circumstances, it is quite natural that when they are now asked to restore an open international system, their own exchange difficulties should at once come to their minds, and that they should think first, not of the opportunities thus to be offered to low-cost producers, but much more of the obligations imposed by membership of such a system to restore the multilateral convertibility of sterling under conditions which cannot now be easily anticipated, and which may be highly embarrassing. In the United States the peculiar difficulties of the immediate post-war transitional period are widely, if perhaps not universally, understood to justify some delay before any movement in this direction was completed, but the earliest possible general restoration of multilateral convertibility is there regarded as axiomatic. For the United States, however, the application of this principle presents no difficult problems, and no one therefore needs to worry very much about it. They know that everybody in other countries is very happy to be paid in dollars. They therefore need feel no concern about the convertibility of their currency, for, so long as the dollar is freely acceptable everywhere, Americans can without any trouble buy anything they want overseas, and a purely hypothetical situation in which this condition would not be satisfied need not be seriously examined.

So far from being hypothetical, however, a similar situation, for the United Kingdom, corresponds exactly with the current facts. Sterling is not to-day everywhere freely acceptable. The United Kingdom authorities therefore feel themselves obliged

65

to husband carefully such foreign exchange resources as are available to them, and the freedom of the British buyer to purchase without limitation in any market that he may choose is necessarily diminished.

Above all the available supply of dollars is much too small to satisfy all the demands which would be forthcoming if the individual purchaser were to be freed from all restraints. In the first instance we naturally enough think of this supply as being inadequate in relation to some traditional level of import requirements. To what extent, if at all, our current difficulties reflect a permanent deterioration in Great Britain's economic position, and how far therefore we may be obliged to take a more modest long-run view of what we can afford to buy from abroad, are questions whose answers depend upon considerations at present largely unknown. Whatever the answers might turn out to be, a plausible case could be made out in theory for attempting to move towards a more stable position, and incidentally to avoid the inconvenience of exchange control, by announcing the free convertibility of sterling, and allowing its value in the foreign exchange market to be determined, and, if necessary, to fall in accordance with current market conditions. At some subsequent stage the risks of such an announcement will have to be taken if an open system is to be re-established, and the long-run objective, in the light of which current decisions ought to be taken, is a state of affairs in which it might safely be assumed that the subsequent movements of the sterling rate of exchange would be negligible. But after such a violent break in continuity as we have recently experienced the risks involved in taking such a decision without the most careful preparation beforehand would be very grave.

This general argument should not be assumed to imply in any way that the restoration of the general multilateral convertibility of national currencies is contrary to long-term British interests. It is not only on account of the importance of her earnings from banking, insurance and entrepôt trade in general, which would be sadly restricted in a bilateralist world, that the United Kingdom has a lively interest in the speedy restoration of multilateral trading. Her chances of taking full advantage of any export opportunities offered by improvements in her own technical efficiency would also be seriously limited if we were unable to buy freely in one market and sell in another. But the consequences of a precipitate and hasty decision to make sterling convertible again might be disastrous. It is not simply a question of issuing a formal announcement on the subject. The convertibility of sterling presupposes the creation of a new set of conditions, and not only of financial conditions in the narrow sense, which could not be established overnight. Many in the United Kingdom, even among those who accept the restoration of multilateral convertibility as an important, or even essential objective, are naturally more acutely conscious of the difficult adaptations which would have to precede and accompany such a restoration than Americans whose troubles are of quite a different kind are likely to be, and there has therefore been a widespread feeling that the United Kingdom should safeguard itself against the risk that it may be manoeuvred, in the interests of a long-range objective which in itself is quite unexceptionable, into a position where she would be obliged to make formal short-term decisions which it would be impossible to maintain.

THE ATTACK ON MULTILATERALISM

What practical conclusions are to be drawn from these various considerations is still a matter for lively dispute. Some would like us to believe that, whatever may be the merits and attractions of an open international system, the peculiar combination of circumstances in which we now find ourselves placed rules it out as a practical possibility. But as the human mind does not easily adjust itself to the unpleasant conclusion that hard facts compel us to embrace a policy which is admittedly second or third rate, there has also been manifest in some quarters a strong tendency to represent the abandonment of the ideas of an open system as something not only imposed by our peculiar difficulties, but actually as good in itself. And to make this idea more attractive, many people begin to question whether multilateral trading was so advantageous or important as we had tended to assume, and this question naturally leads on to statistical studies of the volume of multi-lateral trade.

A considerable amount of ingenuity has been expended in this field, and the results are both interesting and valuable. They are, however, misleading if their results are assumed to afford any useful guide to the practical importance of multi-lateralism. The significance of the fact that holders of foreign currency were free to do as they pleased with it was no less in a case where, say, only 10 per cent of their holdings were spent in countries other than that which had issued the currency, than where the proportion so used was much higher. If it could be shown that for some particular country there was always an exact balancing of debits and credits in relation to every other country, and that therefore statistically there was no triangular or multilateral trade at all, we should still not be justified in assuming that, even for that country, the preservation of the principle of multilateralism was not an important interest. The important thing is the freedom of choice which multilateralism helps to preserve. The position of all the parties concerned, whether directly or indirectly, is fundamentally changed if, on the ground that we have always acted in a certain way in the past, we are to be bound in the future to act in the same way.

It is considerations of this kind which, whether consciously or not, may be presumed to have a considerable influence upon the attitudes of some of the smaller economies towards post-war international economic policy. The re-establishment of an open system is indeed something quite different from the re-establishment of completely free trade, a phrase which strictly speaking has no meaning, as it is impossible to re-establish something which has never existed. We may, if we like, speculate about the theoretical conditions and consequences of completely free trade, but no one seriously supposes to-day that such speculations are likely within any foreseeable future to have much practical significance. But while many of those responsible for economic policy in the smaller economies would probably be very shocked if they were invited to bind themselves to the practice of completely free trade, they are understandably eager to maintain the measure of relative freedom to buy and sell wherever they find it most convenient which the restoration of a multilateral system would ensure. A chronic world shortage of dollars threatens embarrassments for them scarcely less serious than those of which we in Great Britain are now so painfully aware. But to take it for granted that this shortage must be accepted as inevitable for an indefinite period, and therefore to enter into more restricted arrangements of a kind which would threaten to tie up their trade permanently, would for them, be very much like jumping out of the frying-pan into the fire.[1]

Statistical refinements are, in any event, merely a subordinate instrument in the attacks which from a wide variety of quarters have always been directed against the fundamental concept of an "open" system. These attacks have been renewed and intensified in recent years, when vigorous efforts have been made to provide respectable intellectual foundations for the direction of world trade along channels different from those indicated by a comparison of the efficiency of producers, made in the last resort by the considered judgment of the final consumer. It has become fashionable in many quarters to depict international trade in some of its more recent manifestations in the most unfavourable light as "a desperate expedient to maintain employment at home by forcing sales on foreign markets and restricting purchases, which, if successful, will merely shift the problem of unemployment to the neighbour who is worsted in the struggle."[2] The circumstances in which international trade

[1] Swedish attitudes on this question are not necessarily identical with those of other small economies. The views recorded in a report of the Swedish Royal Commission on Post-war Planning of May, 1945, should, nevertheless, be borne in mind in our current speculations about post-war economic policy. "It is definitely in Sweden's interest", it is said, "to develop the freest possible multilateral trade. It goes without saying that Swedish foreign trade will be primarily directed toward those countries where such a tendency is most pronounced, and where it will be able to choose freely the most favourable market . . . . Only in some countries in the world can we venture to count upon such a foreign exchange situation as will enable them to pursue a policy of relatively free trade. It is quite apparent that the markets of these countries will exercise a special attraction over Swedish exports in view of the obvious advantages which trade with such countries offers" (Utredningar angaende Ekonomisk Efterkrigsplanering, IX, pp. 12, 17).
[2] Keynes: *General Theory of Employment, Interest, and Money*, pp. 382-3.

has assumed this appearance are fairly obvious. The much more remarkable thing, however, is the extent to which, even in the most unfavourable conditions, the overwhelming majority of international trade transactions have continued to represent "a willing and unimpeded exchange of goods and services in conditions of mutual advantage."[1] Even at the worst times, the desperate struggle described above was merely a marginal phenomenon on the fringe of the great mass of trade which still conformed broadly speaking to the old principles. Even at a time when commercial policy was greatly influenced by the views of people who professed little respect for the principles of an open system, trade continued to quite a surprising extent to flow along the same channels as would have been prescribed by these principles, and this perhaps provides the clearest proof of the persistent harmony between the principles of an "open" system and the fundamental economic requirements of the world's population.

Without attempting any exhaustive classification of the grounds upon which criticism has been based, we may conveniently distinguish between four distinct, though related, lines of attack. Some of the criticisms which now receive most attention are frequently presented as being modern, but the attacks which still have the greatest practical importance are based on the same set of ideas as for centuries have been used to justify protectionist measures.

Criticisms based upon considerations of national defence have an equally ancient history, and indeed, in principle, no one has ever questioned the hypothesis that in practical decisions affecting commercial policy the overriding interest of national security deserves the most serious attention. In its practical applications, however, this doctrine has often become hopelessly mixed up with straightforward protectionism, and it would be unduly simple-minded to suppose that every plea for a modification of commercial policy which was publicly based upon the defence argument derived its most powerful support from considerations of that kind. Nor is the record of success to be claimed for commercial policies designed to

[1] Keynes: *General Theory of Employment, Interest, and Money*, pp. 382-3.

ensure national security at all impressive. There is, on the contrary, a long list of countries who have endeavoured to protect themselves against the risks of war by trade measures which subsequent events have shown to be entirely ineffective for that purpose. Nevertheless, there can be little doubt that the policies of all governments will continue in the future to be influenced by this objective. The close interrelation between general political security and international economic policy is now a commonplace accepted by everybody. A convenient test of the confidence actually inspired by current arrangements for reconstructing a new international political order will, indeed, be afforded by the actual practice of the states who profess to support it. If in their external economic policy they continue to pay the same attention as in the past to the risks of the recurrence of war, we may safely assume that their confidence has not been significantly increased by the new arrangements.

It has been suggested earlier[1] that when fundamental changes are now asked for in the international economic order, the reasons offered in justification of the change are usually changes in the character of the ends whose achievement is regarded as of the greatest importance or changes in the concrete conditions of production to which the structure of international exchange has to be adapted. Criticism of the principles of an open system has in fact been developed on both these counts. Under the influence of these principles the evolution of world trade tended in the direction of a high degree of international specialization and division of labour, and during the nineteenth and twentieth centuries this was widely believed to be an essential condition for further progress in the efficiency of production, and for the improvements in standards of living which such increased efficiency would normally bring with it. The close integration thereby implied, however, carried with it serious risks of instability. If any economy were closely dependent either for export markets or for supplies of essential goods upon other economies outside its control, any fluctuations in economic activity generated outside were likely to be quickly transmitted to it, and the disadvantages of being submerged

[1] In Chapter IV, p. 44.

71

in the recurrent crises of an unstable world therefore had to be set against the advantages of more efficient production and higher standards of living offered by participation in a growing world economy. Throughout the nineteenth century there was sufficient evidence, though not of quite such a striking character as we have had in recent years, to show that this risk was far from being merely an academic speculation, but at that time most people thought that the risks were worth taking. Now, however, it is commonly said, the balance of opinion is turning or in many countries has already turned in the other direction. The price which the nineteenth century paid for exchange stability and free convertibility was, it is pointed out, the spreading of the international trade cycle, and in the twentieth century more and more people will feel that this price is too high. Stability has become the primary objective of economic policy, and everywhere there is increasing reluctance to run the risks of violent internal fluctuations which a too close association with other economies which cannot be controlled would impose. The elucidation of this issue is indeed the main purpose of this study. Full employment policies are designed to ensure internal stability. The rebuilding of an "open" international economy, it is feared by many, constitutes a threat to this stability. Hence the necessity for an examination of the most effective means of reconciling the two objectives.

It is furthermore frequently argued, not only that there has been a significant change in public opinion on these matters to which public policy must now be made to conform, but also that some of the material conditions upon which the comparative success of the international economic system of the nineteenth century was based have now either disappeared, or else have been radically changed. Whether we like it or not, and quite independently of any changes in public opinion, we must therefore now prepare, so the argument often runs, to abandon any thought of reconstructing the old system, and set out deliberately to build something entirely different.

In any system which has to operate in a changing world it is clearly important to avoid undue rigidity, and we have already seen that flexibility and adaptability to changing circumstances

72

were important conditions for the success of the nineteenth century trading system. Flexibility of that kind now, however, it is commonly argued, will no longer meet the requirements of the case. The changes with which we now have to deal are so fundamental and far-reaching, that nothing less than an entirely new system will suffice. That many far-reaching changes have occurred is indeed obvious enough, and it would be easy to compile a long list of contrasts, each of them significant for a variety of purposes, between the international economic conditions of fifty or a hundred years ago, and those which will confront us in the immediate future. The mere fact of such a change is not, however, by itself sufficient to establish the irrelevance of the principles of an "open" system to the problems of the post-war world. The varied changes in the rates of population growth, for example, are a factor of prime importance for international relations in general, but it is not on the face of it obvious why they should be supposed to have altered in any way the advantages likely to be derived from the localization of production of different kinds in those countries which enjoy the greatest absolute or comparative advantages in each field. The impediments which nearly everywhere now prevent the free movement of labour from one country to another are equally significant for another set of purposes, but again it is not at first sight clear why they should be thought to have diminished the advantages of international division of labour.

On quite a different plane, there is one important respect in which a reconstructed "open" system must almost inevitably differ from its predecessors. The nineteenth century international economic order and the British Constitution were alike in the fact that neither was ever formally embodied in a written document, but developed gradually by a continuous process of trial and error which never reached finality. The nineteenth century gold standard was entirely without any formal constitutional shape, and each country was perfectly free to choose for itself how far it would conform to "the rules of the game". After the dislocations of the inter-war period and the still more violent shocks imposed by the war, it is practically out of the question that a new order of the same flexible character should be reconstituted, with formal responsibilities resting so lightly upon its member states. Institutions of this kind require for their development a period of continuous and uninterrupted growth, and after the sharp breaks of continuity which we have experienced in recent years this condition can probably no longer be satisfied. The creation of the institutions of any new post-war international economic order is in some respects like the construction of a new political unit. Neither can expect to enjoy the blessings of an unwritten constitution, and the commitments involved in adherence to a formal constitution are naturally and properly scrutinized with considerable care.

The contrast between an international order in which the leading role is without dispute reserved for one great economy alone, and an order where responsibility has to be shared, is also of great importance. The restoration of a system in which London would again play an unchallenged leading part is undoubtedly now quite impossible, and it would probably imply too simple a view of the problem to suppose that the United States either could or would merely take over, with such adjustments as changing conditions made necessary, the place occupied before 1914 by the United Kingdom. Many of the troubles of the inter-war period had their origin in failure to appreciate the necessity for adapting traditional practices to new conditions when no single centre any longer commanded the undivided respect formerly accorded to London. The problem, however, is not intrinsically insoluble. Both the structure and the principles of the system will no doubt have to be adjusted to the more complex circumstances which arise when there is no longer a single centre of responsibility, but this does not justify the view that adjustment is impossible.

A more convincing starting-point for the attack on the principles of an "open" system, is, however, frequently sought in a different direction. It is commonly argued that the numerous technical revolutions of recent years have now brought the world to a stage of development where any further benefits likely to accrue from further extensions of international division of labour will be negligible as compared with the benefits likely to arise if each economy established itself in a position where it was free to determine the content of its own internal economic policy without any awkward complications arising from the necessity to have some regard for foreign commercial entanglements. Modern science, it is maintained, has now made it possible to narrow the gap between the efficiencies of production in different countries, so that the losses arising from the concentration of production in the less favoured areas, which the nineteenth century in the conditions then prevailing rightly sought to avoid, would in the new conditions now emerging, be of little practical importance. "One effect of technical progress", it has been said, "is on balance to reduce the margin of comparative cost advantage between the different countries in the production of different commodities . . . In modern conditions, comparative cost advantages can be wiped out by improvements of productive methods and training of labour."[1] "Recent electro-technical and chemical progress tends in the long run to reduce distant trade in raw materials and even foodstuffs . . . . By substituting the ubiquitous and unlimited elements of the chemical world for the localized and scarce products of geological and biological evolution, the new technology seems to hold out, for every well-populated region, a situation of 'productive autarchy'."[2]

By a happy accident, this technological trend appears to harmonize with the still more obvious political trend in the direction of increasing the economic significance of political frontiers, and of confining the movements of resources and goods within national or imperial boundaries. And if it is pointed out, as can very easily be done, that to-day the vast majority of national economies lack the variety and volume of natural resources of all kinds still needed if scientific potentialities are to be converted into realities, the reply is made that the deficiencies of national states can be made good, not by the reconstruction of world economic unity, but rather by expanding existing political units into regional blocs whose resources,

[1] H. W. Arndt: *Economic Lessons of the Nineteen-Thirties*, London, Oxford University Press, 1944, pp. 272-3.
[2] A. Lowe: "The Trend in World Economics", in *American Journal of Sociology*, April 1944, pp. 421-2.

it is hoped, will be so much better "balanced" as to permit us to observe with equanimity a steady decline in the economic relationships between them. Those who are influenced by these views are naturally inclined to take less seriously the risks of conflict between policies motivated by the two objectives which we have been attempting to analyse. For the less highly we rate the benefits likely to accrue from a more elaborate international division of labour, the less will be our alarm at any possible conflict between the two. If in any case these benefits are likely to diminish in importance, we need feel little concern, it is argued, if our efforts to reconcile the two objectives end in failure. At a later stage of our argument[1] we must, therefore, examine this question in more detail, not only in general terms, but also with specific reference to the special problems presented by the peculiar conditions of Great Britain.

Apart from any general considerations which would have had to be taken into account even if there had been no outbreak of war in 1939, no realistic view of the prospects for a new "open" international order at the present time can afford to neglect the consequences of the sharp break in continuity of the basic conditions, technological and financial, which the recent war has imposed upon the world economy. Many of the comparable changes during the nineteenth century were, indeed, sharp enough to cause considerable inconvenience at the time, but most even of the serious adjustments which then had to be made were, so to speak, marginal, and much less far-reaching in their consequences than those which must be made if world trade is again, after the recent war, to settle down along reasonably stable lines. Continuity with the past has not completely disappeared, and much of the experience accumulated before the war concerning differences in relative efficiency will still be valid. But there have been many profound technical changes, the wastage and destruction of capital inevitably for many countries postpones for more than a year or two the time when they can expect to make effective use of their old comparative advantages, and the adaptation of production to war needs has stimulated development in many

[1] In Chapter XI, pp. 172-183.

new directions, not all of which will or should be allowed to wither away now that the war is over. The "pattern" of post-war international economic relations must, for all these reasons, take a shape radically different from that to which we have recently been accustomed, and even if we neglect the possible effects of fluctuating exchange-rates, any current estimate of the post-war competitive position of many economies can be little better than guesswork. The process of determining by trial and error how, under these new and largely unknown conditions, world trade is in future to be allocated, carries with it risks which many people find alarming. There is almost universal agreement that during a transition period of un-determined length it will be impossible to establish policies and institutions which will deserve to be described as "normal".

More important perhaps are, however, the differences of outlook between those who wish to adapt transitional arrange-ments so as to facilitate the eventual reconstruction of a new "open" system in a not too remote future, and those who do not. For it would be misleading to suggest that on this issue there exists anything which could be accurately described as "the" British point of view. Concern about the future British balance of payments may perhaps be said to be universal, and the fear that the real significance of this problem, with all its ramifications, may be inadequately appreciated by those who are not compelled directly to grapple with it is nearly as wide-spread. But there is a highly significant divergence of view between those who insist that temporary arrangements must not be allowed to crystallize into a permanent policy, and those who, it may sometimes be felt, are almost prepared to rejoice over current difficulties as providing an opportunity for establishing a new pattern of trade policy which, in any event, they believe to be superior to any open system.

Those who insist upon the permanent importance of the broad principles revealed by an analysis of the concept of an open international system, are frequently met by the impatient reproach that their approach to current problems is too "nega-tive". They spend too much time, they are told, in criticizing errors to be avoided if the attainment of their ultimate objective is not to be hampered, and too little in formulating positive practical proposals. To identify and to criticize measures likely to conflict with the ultimate objective in view is, indeed, often easier than the elaboration of a detailed practical programme of positive action, but no useful results could be expected from any discussion which evaded a faithful examination of measures which ought to be avoided. In this sense a negative tone is inevitable, nor would any discussion of the most fruitful means for attaining the complementary objective of full employment be helpful which failed to conform to this rule. Especially in the field of international policy, impatience with so-called "negatives" too often conceals a reluctance to clear away some of the obstacles, the maintenance of which would render fruitless many of the measures which arouse enthusiasm and interest on account of their apparent positiveness. It is now common ground among nearly all the academic exponents of full employment policy, that the errors of the Great Depression are to be avoided, and in particular that, in future, no country must seek to "export unemployment" by the restrictive devices which then were so widely adopted. It would, however, demand a degree of *naïveté* verging on blindness to assume that such general declarations were all that was needed to ensure the renunciation of the evil practices of those bad old days. Liberty is not the only noble objective in the name of which the temptation to commit crimes may be overwhelming, and we do well to remind ourselves from time to time that while the phrase "full employment" did not then enjoy the wide popularity now accorded to it, it was actually in the interests of full employment that most of the restrictive devices of the depression were applied. Even if the United States were both to profess and to practise a single-eyed devotion to the objective of full employment, there might still be a long and difficult road to be travelled before the foundations of a stable international economic order were firmly laid. For that very devotion to full employment, the alleged absence of which is so often made a matter of reproach by their critics abroad against both the Administration and the Congress of that country, may too easily be regarded as a justification for a revival of many of the old devices. Objections to the conclusions suggested by an analysis of the implications of an "open" international economic system on the ground of their alleged negative character are, indeed, quite superficial if, as should always be the case, they are merely preliminaries intended to clear the ground for more positive action.

Chapter VI

THE EFFECTS OF MEMBERSHIP OF AN
OPEN INTERNATIONAL ECONOMIC SYSTEM
UPON EMPLOYMENT FLUCTUATIONS
IN GREAT BRITAIN

IN examining the relations, whether harmonious or con-
flicting, between policies designed to achieve either of the
two objectives we have been considering, we might first inquire into the general international conditions which would
have to be satisfied if "full employment" were to be maintained,
and then ask how far, if at all, these conditions were compatible
with the requirements of an open international economy. Or
alternatively after examining the extent to which adherence to
such a system was likely to increase or diminish the risks of
unemployment in Great Britain, and therefore the difficulties
of maintaining "full employment" there, we might proceed
to inquire whether any safeguards could be devised which
would confine these effects within tolerable limits. The final
result should be much the same whichever approach was preferred, but some of the practical issues should be more clearly
outlined if we first see where the second alternative leads us.

If Great Britain is to be an active participant in an "open"
and competitive international economy, it must, as has been
pointed out earlier, be prepared from time to time to adapt
itself to changes which, whether theoretically avoidable or
not, are certain to occur in other parts of the international
economy. More concretely, it must prepare to meet the effects
of fluctuations in the foreign demand for the products of the
British economy of a magnitude which will make desirable
from time to time some awkward transfers of fractions of the
British labour force. There is, of course, no certainty that,
even if repercussions from the world outside could be entirely
excluded, the volume of such transfers required to meet the
consequences of internally generated change would not be
embarrassingly large. But it is precisely for this reason that

80

those likely to be responsible for administering a policy of "full employment" are justifiably anxious lest a close integration with an international economy should increase these difficulties, possibly to such an extent as to create an insoluble problem.

Leaving aside for further consideration later[1] the significance of international trade for British standards of living, we must therefore attempt to classify the more important circumstances in which changes originating abroad are likely to create gaps in the normal British structure of employment. For, if full employment is to be maintained, these gaps will have to be filled by substantial transfers of labour from one sector of employment to another. The changes fall into two main groups, the one associated with more or less permanent changes in the structure of production, as a result of which permanent transfers of part of the labour force must sooner or later be made, the other arising from cyclical fluctuations which might in the course of time be expected to reverse themselves, and the labour adjustments to which might therefore properly be regarded as merely temporary. In recent years, public attention has been concentrated mainly on the consequences of the latter group. There is, however, much to be said for examining the long-term problem first; at the time when the changes occur, it is often extremely difficult to distinguish between the two, and indifference to the necessity for prompt response to the need for long-range adjustment sometimes significantly sharpens the acuteness of the cyclical problem. The cyclical problem will nearly always appear to be more urgent, for it often calls loudly for quick action while long-range adjustments can apparently be more easily postponed. Their importance is therefore likely to be inadequately appreciated, and for that reason we may properly accord to them a higher priority in our classification here than some popular discussions would have led us to expect.

The overseas demand for certain British exports may decline, and the volume of unemployment in export industries and other industries closely associated with them therefore be

[1] In Chapter XI, pp. 176-183.

increased, if rival producers elsewhere get ahead of us in improving their technical efficiency, and are accordingly able to offer more attractive or cheaper goods to our customers abroad. The sharper competition which thus has to be faced may arise as a result either of greater efficiency in those processes in which our exporters have been accustomed to engage, or of the development of new techniques which enable producers in other countries to meet old needs by new methods.

Demand for British exports may also decline as a result of changes in consumers' demand which reflect changes in fashion or in popular taste. Unless these are closely linked up with technological changes, as they often are, their effects are likely to be felt rather gradually. They may, however, be highly embarrassing if we enter into arrangements which, whether so intended or not, have the effect of concealing from us the earliest indications of a downward trend of demand. These indications should be welcomed as showing the direction in which adjustments will soon be needed.

There are, however, some significant similarities between the effects of changes of this kind and the effects of changes of commercial policy, which in a sense reflect the combined judgment of consumers as to the sources from which it is best to satisfy some of their requirements. The demand for British exports, and therefore the volume of British employment, is liable to be affected by movements in foreign tariffs, by changes in the administration of foreign exchange controls, or by changes in the internal or external values of foreign currencies, which at least temporarily alter the competitive strength of rival producers elsewhere, independently of any change in their comparative technical efficiency.

Under each of the headings mentioned above, the demand for British exports might fall because for one reason or another some of our customers wished to buy other things in preference to our exports. But their demand might also decline because, whatever their preferences might be, they were unable on account of a fall in their income to give effect to them. This might, in part, be the result of a long-term deterioration in their economic position, or, as in normal times would be more probable, of failure on the part of themselves or their governments to control the vagaries of the trade cycle.

The fear of instability arising in this way is probably the most important influence at work in the minds of those who now hesitate about the wisdom of re-establishing close connections between the British economy and other economies, particularly the United States, which are liable to violent fluctuations. In estimating the volume of employment at which Great Britain should aim after the war, Sir William Beveridge has set down "1 per cent of unemployment each year on an average of all years together" as what he described as "the price paid for the advantages of international trade."[1] This figure, however, contrasts so sharply with the actual record of the inter-war period, that it could probably be realized only if we could assume a reformation in other countries' economic policies at least as great, and perhaps even more far-reaching than that which we proclaim our intention of enforcing in our own.[2] The United States is not the only country the stability of whose demand for imports is important for the stability of the British economy, but it is particularly in connection with this problem, that United States policy attracts a very large share of our attention. For not only is the United States' share in world production and in the demand for the basic materials which are so important in world trade very great, but, during the inter-war period, the amplitude and vigour of industrial fluctuations were considerably more pronounced in that country than in most other parts of the world. During this period, too, United States imports usually fluctuated even more widely than national income, and these exaggerated movements in the United States demand for foreign goods both directly and indirectly increased the risks of unemployment in other countries. Leaving out of account the abnormal transactions of the years immediately following the war of 1914-18, it is significant to recall that the supply of dollars available to the rest of the world, mainly as a result of

[1] Beveridge, *Full Employment in a Free Society*, p. 128.
[2] cf. E. A. G. Robinson, "Sir William Beveridge on Full Employment" *Economic Journal*, April 1945.

United States purchase of imports and of United States foreign investments, rose steadily year by year, from $4,853 millions in 1921 to $7,507 millions in 1928, but by 1933 had fallen precipitately to $2,367 millions. The impact of these violent fluctuations upon other countries was disastrous, and it is not surprising that many are reluctant to place themselves in a position where a similar disaster might recur. As one United States writer has put it, "A world economic structure organized on the basis of equal treatment and with large scope for free enterprise, cannot be maintained in the face of such reductions in the supply of dollars as have occurred in our international transactions in the past."[1]

Closely connected with the fluctuations of the trade cycle, but sufficiently important to be listed separately, is the effect on the one hand of fluctuations in the volume of foreign investment, and on the other of fluctuations in the returns from foreign investments made in the past. Especially where employment is to any significant extent dependent upon the continuous export of capital goods, any interruption in the flow of international investment will increase the difficulties of maintaining employment at a satisfactory level, while a sudden decline in income from foreign investments will upset the balance of payments, and thereby make it more difficult to maintain stable relations between employment in export and in other industries. The policy of the United States has historically been of great importance in connection with both these points. It is now the world's leading creditor nation, but the growth of its overseas assets has been erratic in a high degree. From 1919 to 1929 loans floated in the United States provided a net addition of $7,500 millions to the capital of foreign countries, a total larger than the combined foreign investments of all other capital-lending countries during the same period. But after 1929 the stream of American foreign investment practically dried up, and there was instead a heavy net inflow of capital into the United States from other countries. United States policy cannot be held solely responsible for fluctuations

[1] Foreword to Hal B. Lary and associates, *The United States in the World Economy*, United States Department of Commerce, 1943, p. vi.

in the capacity of debtor countries to meet their overseas liabilities. Many of them were guilty of serious errors of judgment which sooner or later were sure to land them in grave difficulties. But the widespread failure of foreign debtors to meet their obligations during the Great Depression would not have gone nearly so far if the United States had been more successful in restraining within reasonable limits its own internal fluctuations.

The influence of each of the factors which have been mentioned could easily be illustrated in much greater detail from the history of the inter-war period, and the story would also remind us how difficult it often was at the time to distinguish clearly between the effects of the different elements in the situation. We may recall, for example, the lively disputes about the relative importance of the parts played by a depreciating yen and by increased productive efficiency in the more intense competition from Japanese textile producers, which so much embarrassed the Lancashire cotton industry, while the steep decline in the national income of the United States, which was such a violently destabilizing factor for the rest of the world, also probably had its origin, at least to some extent, in technological changes and the failure to make prompt structural adjustments to meet them, as well as in the more obvious causes of cyclical fluctuation. And especially in making the necessary transitional post-war adjustments in the structure of British trade and industry, each of the factors mentioned must be taken into account in deciding the course most likely to be effective for reviving British export trade, whatever long-run international economic policy may be thought most appropriate for this country. Will synthetic rubber prove an adequate substitute for the natural product? Will Latin-American consumers who used to buy British goods have lost their taste for them as a result of the inability of British producers to supply their needs during the war? Will Australia insist upon permanent protection for the new industries which have expanded in that country to meet wartime needs? Will the income level of the devastated countries of Europe remain so low that their demand for some of the British exports which they were glad to purchase before the war will for a long time be negligible? Will any American investors who enter the international field repeat the extravagances of the nineteen-thirties and then suddenly cut down on their foreign lending, or will their post-war investment be more delicately adjusted to the basic requirements of an expanding world economy? Obviously, no one of these questions is easy to answer, and they are merely typical specimens from a list which could without difficulty be extended almost indefinitely.

It has now become the common, and for many purposes convenient, practice to describe the problems with which we have been dealing, in terms of maladjusted balances of payments. It may, however, be worth while to recall the elementary fact, which an incautious reader of technical discussions of the balance of payments might sometimes overlook, that if the balance of payments gets out of gear as a result of inadequate demand for our exports, the central problem, of which the disordered balance of payments is merely a symptom, is, in fact, the problem of diminishing employment opportunity. A variety of devices might be used to correct maladjusted balances of payments, and we should not be so timidly cautious as to reject out of hand any suggestion for temporary financial relief as merely postponing the more radical solutions which will ultimately be necessary. The breathing space which such temporary relief would afford might be very useful if we used it vigorously and intelligently. It is also true that the significance of balance of payment troubles extends a good deal further than this. A chronically unbalanced situation would threaten the stability of our currency, and whatever immediate effects this might have on our employment position, a long-range employment policy must also aim at providing some protection against these risks. The fundamental fact remains that so long as the demand for our exports is deficient, we are likely to have an unemployment problem, whatever we may think it proper to do about the balance of payments.

Chapter VII

INTERNATIONAL CONDITIONS FOR
THE MAINTENANCE OF FULL EMPLOYMENT

IF it is to be applicable to economies of every type, any statement of the international conditions to be satisfied if an internal policy of full employment is to be successful must inevitably be cast in very general terms, which will require adaptation before the analysis is applied to any individual economy. Even if we are agreed about the general principles, there may still be difficulty in getting agreement about their application to particular cases.

Most of the current discussion in Great Britain to-day starts from the hypothesis that full employment can best be attained and maintained by using a combination of cheap money with government action of various kinds to maintain an adequate volume of investment and thus to keep up the level of effective demand. There will therefore be less risk of our analysis being purely academic if we first inquire what international conditions must be satisfied if a policy of this kind is not to encounter serious difficulties in the international field. We must, however, also bear in mind throughout that these conditions will be affected by the proportions in which we propose to combine all the various ingredients of a full employment policy, no less than by their specific content.

MAINTENANCE OF ADEQUATE EXPORT DEMAND

The primary international condition for the maintenance of full employment by these means is the maintenance of the demand for the principal kinds of exports at a level sufficiently stable to ensure that the strain placed at any time upon our capacity for adjusting the employment structure of the country shall not be too severe. We must also take into account the general overriding condition that our balance of payments shall be protected from either short or long-term disturbances greater than the economy can stand. This condition is, indeed, important whether or not we have a full employment policy, but it demands particularly careful attention when the maintenance of a high level of employment is made a deliberate objective of policy. For if the level of effective demand is maintained by any of the methods described in an earlier section, our demand for imports will inevitably be affected. The precise character of the additional demand cannot easily be forecast in detail, but it seems reasonable to assume that those whose money income is increased by a full employment policy will use a part of the increase, the size of which may be predicted from observation of the current expenditure habits of comparable income groups, for the purchase of additional imports.[1] Unless the foreign demand for our exports—subject to the usual qualifications about the so-called "invisible" items—is somehow or other adjusted to the import demand thus sustained or raised, the normal balance of payments will be destroyed.

The avoidance of abrupt variations in the demand for our exports depends upon a number of conditions. The ability of other economies to control trade cycle fluctuations has attracted most attention in current discussions of this problem, and on any hypothesis must be regarded as an issue of first-rate importance. It is still a centre of lively controversy, but even those who might dispute whether, in the last resort, the measures of stabilization which were practicable deserved to be described as measures for "controlling" the trade cycle, would usually not deny that the fluctuations of the past had been unnecessarily violent and extensive, and that in the future we might by wise policy mitigate them to such an extent that any cyclical disturbances still unavoidably remaining would no longer present a problem of first-rate importance.

A factor closely related to, but not identical with, the fluctuations of the trade cycle is the level of expenditure in the

[1] Statistical calculations have been attempted with a view to estimating more precisely the probable size of this share. Mr Kaldor, for example, states that "under the conditions of the 1930s, a £100 increase (or decrease) in the national income, caused a £15 increase (or decrease) of imports" (Beveridge, *Full Employment in a Free Society*, p. 358). But such calculations, however refined, seem unlikely to offer more than the roughest guidance for the future, as it is scarcely possible to forecast how far demand for imports may be affected by influences not directly associated with movements in aggregate national income.

principal countries to which we hope to sell our exports. If our full employment policy is not to encounter serious international difficulties it is therefore also desirable that, irrespective of trade cycle fluctuations, effective steps should be taken to avoid disturbing variations, due to other causes, in the level of expenditure in these countries.

Both these conditions would apparently be most easily satisfied if all the economies whose fluctuations might be damaging to employment in Great Britain were to be found by common consent applying policies which would incidentally keep their demand for British exports at a satisfactory level. And as such a happy coincidence is unlikely to be the result of mere chance, there has been strong support for efforts to persuade other economies to adopt internal policies similar to those which we approve for ourselves. The suggestion has been made that an international conference might produce generally acceptable rules of policy with sufficient binding force to afford adequate guarantees against the risk of internationally generated fluctuations. The formal acceptance of general principles is, however, notoriously no guarantee that they will in fact be practised; some therefore have gone a good deal further and maintained in effect that we should reserve our judgement in regard to any commitments proposed to us in the field of international economic policy until we had actually seen how successful other economies were in maintaining full employment.[1]

When we talk about the international conditions for the maintenance of full employment, it is of course again the post-war policy of the United States which we have most in mind. The phrase, full employment, is indeed used almost as freely in the United States as it is in Great Britain, and discussions of various

---

[1] Sir William Beveridge, for example, declared that "it is necessary that the major participating countries should not merely aim at full employment, but should in practice secure it or secure something like it." (*Full Employment in a Free Society*, p. 225.) The realization of this condition, he declared to be necessary "to ensure the continuance of multilateral trading", and the general tone of his argument implied that if it could not be satisfied, the effort to reconstruct a world-wide multilateral trading system would have to be abandoned. As in the nature of things, the maintenance of full employment must be a continuing process which can never be declared complete, the acceptance of these views would leave it open to a sceptic to press for the postponement of any such effort until an indefinitely remote future.

full employment policies have been scarcely less vigorous there than those to which British readers are now accustomed. Many important sections of United States opinion do not, however, favour the kind of solution which is now most widely approved in Great Britain, and much of the coolness which some in this country have displayed towards proposals to reconstitute an open international system arises from the pessimistic views which they take of the probability that these sections of United States opinion will dominate United States policy, and that the American economy will therefore again be as violently unstable as it was before 1939. But the very fact that the risks of post-war instability in the United States may be abnormally high obliges us to take particular care that we do not ask for more from that country than is absolutely necessary for the general purpose in view. Even if it were on all counts desirable that the United States should adopt full employment techniques similar to our own, with suitable modifications to suit the circumstances of that country, it would still be proper to inquire whether the embarrassments threatened by United States instability might not be sufficiently avoided by less far-reaching measures. In the long run no doubt the highest degree of prosperity in the United States, as indeed in most other countries, is an important British interest, but even if the normal level of employment in the United States were, for example, well below Sir William Beveridge's objective of 97 per cent, the international conditions which for us in Great Britain are relevant to the maintenance of full employment might still be quite favourable. Provided that it did not fluctuate too much, a level of production in the United States substantially lower than was technically possible need not seriously affect the British employment situation. The concrete conditions which are really important for us are that the dollar supply available for the rest of the world should be reasonably stable, and that the United States should maintain a long-term balance in its international transactions; a sufficient approximation to these conditions would be possible even if the United States failed to attain full employment in any of the senses in which that phrase is commonly used in this country.

But while we may be asking for more than we really need if we insist upon the general adoption elsewhere of employment policies broadly similar to our own, it is also possible that uniformity of national practice in this sphere would not suffice to safeguard us against all serious difficulties. There is no necessary uniformity in the movements of the price level which would in different countries be adequate to stimulate a satisfactory level of employment or in the effects of the attainment of such a level upon the demand for imports. Even if we were assured of the most effective co-ordination of national policies, all motivated by the same purpose and all based upon broadly similar techniques, it might still be necessary, before international equilibrium could finally be attained, for us to make structural adjustments on a scale larger than we cared to face, and this would be the more probable if our own interpretation of full employment leaned too heavily in the direction of avoiding substantial structural shifts of employment.

Still more important, even after full employment had once been attained in all the main economies, it could not be maintained unless from time to time we adapted our economic structure to long-term changes in the basic international conditions of production; these changes, by varying the customary demand for our exports, would sometimes oblige us to undertake shifts in employment which might be very embarrassing for us. Our full employment policy would therefore encounter much less difficulty if the further international condition were satisfied that structural changes in world production as a whole should be such that the task of adapting our economy to the new conditions thus created should not be too difficult.

The general acceptance of an appropriate policy for fixing the external values of national currencies is also of great practical importance, though this condition stands on a different plane from those which we have so far discussed. In any analysis of the causes of the international economic troubles of the inter-war period misunderstandings of the importance of this point must be given a high place. In 1918 it was taken for granted that the speedy restoration of the pre-1914 sterling-dollar exchange rate was an overriding objective to which priority over all other considerations was properly to be given. There is now wide-spread agreement that this belief fundamentally misconceived the new situation which had arisen, pre-1914 exchange rates no longer having any significant relationship with post-1918 facts. The mistake then made with regard to sterling was, however, only one, though no doubt practically the most important, illustration of the general problem of determining the proper external value of national currencies. No international economic system can function smoothly if the external values of national currencies as expressed in current rates of exchange are badly out of alignment with internal price and cost structures, and there would necessarily in such circumstances be serious difficulties in maintaining satisfactorily stable employment levels.

STABILITY IN BALANCE OF PAYMENTS

The international conditions which must be satisfied if undue disturbances in our balance of payments are to be avoided are to a large extent identical with those which we have just examined. In general an internal full employment policy would be frustrated if long-run equilibrium could not be maintained in the balance of payments without resorting to deflation, such as would necessitate some contraction of internal activity, or perhaps indeed without damping down the rate of credit expansion, the maintenance of which is on some hypotheses believed to be necessary for the maintenance of full employment. And it will also be difficult to maintain employment at an adequate level if in the short run there should be a deterioration in the balance of payments so sudden or so drastic that its effects upon employment could not be adequately offset by changes in the volume or direction of internal investment. National full employment policies of the kind which we have been discussing would therefore require the backing of an international economic system which provided proper facilities for realizing these conditions.

In this context an appropriate policy for determining exchange rates is of particular importance. Moreover, even if other countries adopted full employment policies which were shown by experience to be reasonably effective, situations would still probably arise from time to time, though it might be hoped less frequently than in the past, when the maintenance of equilibrium in our balance of payments would, if rules similar to those of the old gold standard were still in force, require deflationary action from us, and therefore threaten unemployment. Especially in recent years many economies in such a situation have preferred the relief afforded by a depreciated exchange rate to the harshness of deflation. There are differences of opinion about the adequacy of such currency devaluation as an instrument for dealing with these situations, but even those who rate it low would usually agree that it might sometimes be useful as a supplementary or reserve measure. In listing the international conditions for the maintenance of full employment, this question, however, has two aspects. With a view to maintaining its own freedom of action, each economy might press for a general recognition of the respectability of devaluation in appropriate circumstances. But our own stability might be endangered by too free a use by others of this right, and it is therefore equally important to insist that variations in exchange rates are not matters of exclusively domestic concern, and should be subject to review of some kind by an appropriate international authority. Acceptance of the general principle that agreed variations in exchange rates might sometimes be permitted as a safeguard against threatened disequilibrium in the balance of payments does not indeed mean that in any particular case agreement will necessarily be forthcoming. We have little experience of the practical working of conventions of conduct in this sphere, for the precedent of the pre-war tripartite monetary agreement was set in peculiar circumstances which may not recur. Even if the prospects for agreement were good, many would still dislike exchange depreciation, partly for reasons of prestige, and partly because they would fear that a depreciated exchange rate might cause a grave deterioration in their terms of trade. Though the confident belief may be unjustified, or at least greatly exaggerated, that an economy threatened by disequilibrium in its balance of payments would place itself in a stronger bargaining position by imposing exchange control instead of depreciating its exchange rate, it will still be necessary in such circumstances to safeguard ourselves against the pressure for the application of exchange controls and other similar restrictive measures to correct any disequilibrium which may arise.

Undue disturbances in the balance of payments will also occur if we cannot avoid violent fluctuations in either short or long-term capital movements. As we have already seen, certain types of full employment policy are likely to expand our demand for imports without necessarily having any correspondingly favourable effect upon our position as an exporter; in these circumstances the accumulation of international reserves on a scale sufficient to enable us to face without alarm the consequences of temporary transfers of capital might be much more difficult than it would have been if our demand for imports had not thus been inflated. The balancing of debits and credits in our international accounts would therefore be an unusually delicate business, easily upset by even quite modest movements of capital. For this reason, among others, the administrators of national full employment programmes are likely to look with special care either for assurances that embarrassing capital movements will not occur, or alternatively that if such movements seem probable they will be allowed a reasonably free hand to control them.

PROGRESS IN PRODUCTIVE EFFICIENCY

One important overall factor, the relative progress of productive efficiency in this country as compared with our competitors, will also operate continuously either to increase or to diminish the acuteness of our difficulties under any of the heads which we have mentioned. A high level of employment might emerge as, so to speak, a by-product of a rapidly expanding economy in which technological progress combined with a high degree of mobility of resources of production to ensure a steady improvement in both the efficiency of production and the standard of living. If in particular productive efficiency in the export sector increased more in Great Britain than in competing countries there would be a tendency for our share of exports to increase, and this would help to offset the effect of any other adverse factors and enable us to finance the additional import demand generated by rising standards of living. Increased efficiency might moreover justify us, even on the basis of a strict comparison of costs, in replacing some of our traditional imports by goods produced at home. If, on the other hand, the rate of increase of our productivity were less than that of competing countries, all our difficulties would be exaggerated. And since at the present time we in Great Britain start from a position in which we cannot even restore our pre-war standard of living without an increase in exports which connotes a sharp improvement in our productivity relative to that of competing countries, this factor is of peculiar importance for us.

A deterioration in our relative productive capacity is not, however, the only possible reason why from time to time we may find increasing difficulty in maintaining the level of exports which our economy needs. Even if the standard of technical efficiency in every section of the export trade of the United Kingdom were thoroughly satisfactory, we should still in our present peculiar circumstances be obliged to give to export policy the most careful consideration. The maintenance of exports must inevitably be a continuing pre-occupation in any economy which was able to press ahead with a full employment policy more vigorously and more successfully than its partners in an international economic system, and the maintenance of even the highest technical standards would not necessarily safeguard us against all the disturbing effects of long-range diversions of consumers' demand.

What in broad outline should be our policy in face of difficulties such as these? It should go without saying that in all such circumstances the maintenance of our standards of efficiency at the highest possible level is an urgent necessity. By the installation of more modern machinery, the adoption of improved techniques of production, or the improvement of managerial methods, there is usually always some scope for significant cost reduction. It would not, however, necessarily be discreditable to our industry if in certain circumstances its utmost endeavours to raise the level of technical efficiency should be inadequate to assure the established position in export markets that is desired, and in that event some of those whose responsibility it is to sell goods abroad will naturally from time to time look in other directions for the means of strengthening their competitive position.

THE PROBLEM OF COMPETITIVE EXPORTS

It will always be easier to maintain a satisfactory level of exports if world conditions in general are favourable to economic expansion. With the volume of exports as a whole expanding rapidly, there will then be no strong urge to wrest export trade away from other people. But even in the most favourable circumstances much of our export is certain to be competitive, and some of it highly competitive with the exports of other countries. Wherever or whenever the margin in our favour becomes uncomfortably narrow, there may well be a strong tendency to press for wage reductions as superficially the most obvious way of cutting costs and strengthening the competitive position of British exporters in overseas markets. If this were the proper path to follow, the problem might be regarded as a matter of purely internal concern, except so far as wage cuts might provoke reactions in other countries which would contract our export outlets. Apart, however, from any other consideration which might properly be regarded as relevant, there would also be an obvious unfairness in expecting those who happened to be employed in an export industry to bear the whole of the consequences of Great Britain's competitive weakness, and to submit to a relatively lower standard of real income than was enjoyed by others to whom fortune had given employment in some more sheltered field. Equity demands that any sacrifices which in the interests of the economy as a whole may be needed in the struggle for a firmer position in export markets should be more widely shared. Under conditions approximating to full employment the bargaining position of wage-earners would moreover be very strong, and it would be extremely difficult either to persuade or to compel wage-earners in particular export industries to submit to radical changes in what had come to be generally accepted as the normal wage-structure of the economy as a whole.

It is in circumstances such as these that the case for depreciation of the external value of the national currency has to many people seemed particularly strong, and depreciations which did not provoke reprisals would scarcely be possible unless favourable international conditions were assured. A devaluation of the currency is, at the time it is made, in effect equivalent to the imposition of a flat *ad valorem* duty on all imports and the payment of a subsidy on all exports. It is therefore likely to protect the balance of payments, and at the same time to provide a breathing space within which such structural adjustments as the economy may need can be carried through in an orderly manner. This argument has often been most forcibly presented from the point of view of primary producing countries with an unusually high degree of dependence upon a few staple exports. " 'A fundamental disequilibrium', " it has been stated, "may be corrected most satisfactorily by a variation of the exchange rate. . . . It avoids the worst and most distressing features of deflation, it keeps trade free of special restrictions and quotas, and provides the quickest and least disturbing method of making a fundamental adjustment",[1] though we might add that it may also give undue encouragement to some of those who in any case will be reluctant to see the necessity for readjustment.

It is unfortunately not always easy at the time to know for certain whether the difficulties encountered by exporters are merely temporary or attributable to a "fundamental disequilibrium". In any given case, moreover, the probable effects of devaluation upon the balance of payments will depend upon the elasticities of demand for both exports and imports. Statistical forecasts in this field are unusually difficult and speculative, and confident conclusions cannot be based upon their results. It certainly cannot yet be regarded as firmly established that the elasticities most relevant for Great Britain would be sufficiently favourable to warrant any expectation that even in the long run a devaluation of sterling would ensure stability for the British economy. Even if the immediate effects on balance seemed likely

[1] D. B. Copland, *The Road to High Employment*, Cambridge, Massachusetts, Harvard University Press, 1945, p. 89.

to be favourable to us, the stimulus given to our exports would also necessarily be undiscriminating, a fact which would increase the risks of resentment and reprisals abroad. There is no certainty that the depreciation of sterling would be well received in the United States; we should also take into account its effects upon the value of our earnings on invisible items, and we could not afford to neglect the interests of countries which during the war have been obliged to accumulate large sterling balances. For these and other reasons many have been disposed to favour as protective measures against the risks of an unfavourable balance of payments policies adjusted more discriminatingly to the requirements of different industries. These would include export subsidies and special exchange rates, of the kind which will be rejected as inadmissible, or at least very severely restricted, if the project for an international code of conduct for national commercial policies is worked out on the basis of a multilateral world trading system.

At a later stage of our argument something more of a general character will be said about these issues. Here it will suffice to say that if we assume on the one hand that by adopting full employment techniques we rule out the deflationary effects of variations in the national level of economic activity, and on the other that the trend of international negotiations on economic policy continues to follow the course at present marked out for them, the most important way of escape allowed to us, if the export difficulties which we have described threaten to become acute, will be provided in the first instance by access to the credit facilities of the International Monetary Fund, and ultimately by the right in certain agreed circumstances to devalue our currency.

It is, however, still more important to insist that while we may properly seek for temporary relief while adjusting our economy to changes in relative productive efficiency, it will in the long run, and often in the short run too, be impossible to protect ourselves from either relative or absolute declines in our real income by any method other than efficient production. "Under no system of monetary policy", or, we might add, of any other kind of policy either, "can things be very pleasant for a country which finds the productivity of other countries in *competitive goods* increasing faster than its own."[1]

This does not mean, however, that if things go badly for us we must allow real incomes to fall while we cling grimly to the remnants of our declining traditional export trades. We can still in these circumstances protect our standards of living if we can find alternative relatively new exports in which our competitive position is stronger. This has been our normal practice in the past, a practice moreover invariably followed by every country which has been successful in maintaining or improving a strong export position in world markets. If, as seems probable, our own current position demands adjustments of this kind on a wider scale than we have usually found necessary in the past, the point to which we have directed attention several times in the course of our argument, the necessity for the utmost flexibility in the structure of our production, is clearly seen to be of overwhelming importance.

It may be too much to expect that the combined effects of all the changes in productive efficiency which are likely to occur will be to establish just that happy balance which would suit us best, but on the whole the more reliance we can place upon improvements in the efficiency of our own production, and upon the flexibility of our own economic structure, the less will be the risks of our having to face either intractable unemployment difficulties or disrupting disturbances in our balance of payments. In particular, unremitting attention to the general conditions of productive efficiency will widen the bottlenecks where the pressure towards an upward movement of prices is likely first to be felt, and will therefore diminish the difficulties of maintaining a proper relationship between our own price level and those of other countries, which are often likely to be at the root of any balance-of-payments disequilibria threatened by the pursuit of full employment in a single economy.

If other economies are sluggish in transferring resources of production from one field to another, the temptation to protect established positions by restrictive measures which threaten

[1] D. H. Robertson, *International Gold Problem*, London, Oxford University Press, 1931, p. 46.

unemployment in Great Britain may be very great. In general, therefore, a high degree of flexibility in other economies is also an important British interest. The greater their success in widening any bottlenecks and loosening any rigidities which would otherwise impede their normal growth, the weaker will be the incentive to cut down their demand for our exports. The view could therefore be plausibly defended that the most important "international condition" for the maintenance of full employment in Great Britain would be the widest possible adoption in other countries of measures which were likely to have this effect. The most determined opposition to any radical reform of the United States tariff, for example, is rooted in the strength of the interests which resist the profound readjustments needed if the cost structure of certain sectors of United States agriculture is to be brought into line with the general world price situation. A frontal attack on these interests has at best only doubtful prospects of success, but the position would be substantially improved if some of those now employed in these protected sectors found that it was easier than it had been in the past to transfer to other parts of the economy. Our own difficulties in maintaining a high level of employment, whether internal or international, will be diminished by such success as we can register in widening within our economy the bottlenecks which usually appear whenever a policy of expansion is vigorously pressed. The maintenance of international equilibrium will similarly be made easier if other economies are also careful to check the development of similar bottlenecks, and this is equally true whether or not they make full employment a deliberate objective of policy.

The possibility should not, however, be ignored, that from the standpoint of our own convenience other economies might be embarrassingly vigorous in maintaining a high degree of flexibility. If in general other economies were much more flexible than ours, if in particular they gave a much more prominent place than we thought necessary or found convenient to measures for making structural adjustment easy as a means for stabilizing employment at a high level, we might find ourselves confronted with the necessity for arranging for transfers of labour on an embarrassingly large scale. This, however, is clearly a matter upon which it would be unreasonable for us, merely in the interests of greater stability for ourselves, to ask other economies to limit their freedom of action. And this is one of the reasons why even a watertight international agreement to maintain full employment everywhere might not in all conceivable circumstances suffice to provide international conditions which would guarantee the maintenance of full employment in Great Britain.

THE SIGNIFICANCE OF TRADE BARRIERS

There is one other field of international policy, whose bearing upon full employment has been much disputed, and upon which some general observations may appropriately be made here. To what extent, if at all, is a general relaxation of trade barriers also a significant international condition for the maintenance of full employment? There is now at least formal general agreement that on other grounds some relaxation of this kind is desirable, but it has been strongly argued that, in relation to employment policy, it is a matter of quite subordinate importance. An assurance of full employment, it is maintained, is an essential condition for the acceptance of freer commercial policies rather than the other way round. It is indeed both true and important that the defence of trade restrictions is usually more tenacious when general economic conditions are depressed, than when the outlook for future expansion is bright, but it is nevertheless a mistake, in this as in so many other contexts, to think of two objectives, both of which are in themselves highly desirable, as if one of them were always to be given priority over the other. We should, indeed, be greatly embarrassed if we were informed by the Government of the United States that we might choose between a high and stable level of employment in that country and a radical reform of its tariff and commercial policy, but could not have both. A most persuasive case could be made out for the view that we should be wise to select the former alternative, but our confidence in this choice might be weakened as we reflected upon the high degree of probability that political pressures might make further trade restrictions appear a very attractive weapon for the United States in any determined attack upon unemployment. Happily, in real life it is inconceivable that such a simple choice would ever present itself, and the attractiveness of trade restrictions as a means for guaranteeing employment is traditionally so great that we could never afford to disclaim all interest in the commercial policies of other countries. For an economy in a situation such as that of post-war Britain, a general lowering of trade barriers may not be, in the strict sense of the term, an international condition for the maintenance of full employment. If, however, that condition were actually realized, we should certainly find it much easier to get through the difficulties of the transitional period, and to establish more normal conditions in which we might reasonably expect to be able to maintain stable levels of employment, without constant recourse to emergency measures.

The international "implications" of full employment are wider than the "international conditions" to be satisfied if national full employment policies are not to be frustrated.[1] The effort to attain full employment may itself impede the evolution of satisfactory international economic relations, if those responsible for it are too inclined to interpret full employment as meaning that people should be guaranteed the particular jobs which they already happen to have. For they will then be tempted to achieve their objective by restrictive protectionist devices, whether of the old-fashioned type, or of the more refined kind which were widely used during the inter-war period. If insistence upon occupational security makes our national economic structure very rigid, the pressure to protect it by more elaborate barriers to foreign trade against the impact of new foreign products and reduced real costs, and to use export subsidies to bolster up industries the foreign demand for whose products had declined, may be very strong, and all this is very likely to provoke retaliation and further restrictions

[1] A more elaborate analysis of the International Monetary Implications of National Anti-Depression Policy, is to be found in Chapter XVII of *Economic Stability in the Post-War World*, Report of the Delegation on Economic Depressions, Part II, League of Nations, 1945.

in international trade. It is of little avail to argue that restrictions upon foreign trade will more easily be removed after national economies have achieved full employment, if to any substantial extent the foundations of full employment have been laid in policies which presuppose the maintenance of restrictions upon foreign trade. The inter-war period was full of illustrations of these tendencies and the whole history of the last pre-war decade might, with but little oversimplification, be told as the story of unco-ordinated and usually unsuccessful efforts to check the decline of employment by the piecemeal use of such devices. It may reasonably be hoped that a long-term full employment policy might avoid some of the short-sighted errors which the hastiness of the efforts of the nineteen-thirties to ensure protection against the combined pressure of technological change and widespread deflation made almost inevitable. Nevertheless, any country which aims at full employment, but is at the same time reluctant to break down the traditional rigidities in its economic structure, is likely in the course of time to become gradually less and less dependent on external trade, sacrificing to occupational security some of the benefits to be obtained from full participation in international division of labour. If other economies can be found in which the desire for occupational security is equally strong, the sacrifice may be reduced by quantitative trade agreements with mutual obligations to continue an agreed volume of purchases over a period of time. The inevitable rigidity of such arrangements is likely, however, to mean that full enjoyment of the benefits of technical progress is delayed and perhaps indefinitely postponed, while the weaker partner in such an agreement is always in some danger of finding himself at a serious disadvantage in striking a bargain.

Chapter VIII

SAFEGUARDS AGAINST EMPLOYMENT FLUCTUATIONS ARISING FROM INTERNATIONAL ECONOMIC CONNECTIONS

UPON certain types of mind with a natural eagerness to experiment with the unknown, the effect of a catalogue of uncertainties such as we have presented in Chapter VI might be positively invigorating. It can, however, scarcely be a matter for surprise that in a world which has, throughout a whole generation, been obliged to move unceasingly from one bewildering set of uncertainties to another, many should now feel impelled by the strongest possible motives to seek for assured safeguards against any repetition of this unhappy experience. For some, this search leads to speculation about the possibility of at least a partial withdrawal from a troublous and turbulent world and the construction of a more orderly economic system within relatively restricted geographical limits, and the character of such a hypothetical system tends to be much the same whether its sponsors are moved mainly by a natural timidity or rather by an excessive confidence in their ability to control the destinies of the new order which they hope to construct. It will, however, be more convenient at this stage of our argument to leave these speculations on one side, and to examine first the safeguards which might be available without sacrificing the essential elements of a genuine international system.

There is nothing at all unreasonable about a search for safeguards of this kind, and no serious harm is likely to be done if, in the first instance, we aim rather higher than subsequently we may find it possible to attain. Nevertheless, the search should be prosecuted with a full appreciation of the fact that even for the most powerful or the most skilfully ordered economy, there can never be any final or absolute protection against all the risks of a changing world. In our highly complex and suspicious

104

international society, no economy can reasonably hope for watertight guarantees which would afford anything like complete protection against the risks of the disruptive impact of unfavourable events in the world outside.

There is, indeed, some danger that a too-anxious preoccupation with safeguards may sometimes actually increase the chance that the evils against which protection is being sought will be converted from mere possibilities into realities; if our interest in safeguards leads us to spend too much time in speculating about an imaginary world in which everything was neatly arranged in accordance with our views of our own convenience, we may encourage the growth of an unhealthy state of mind in which it would become increasingly difficult firmly and resolutely to face the harsh facts. Nevertheless, we should also be careful not to fall into the opposite error of assuming that we are helpless in the face of inexorable forces beyond our control. The very fact that there have been radical and unprecedented changes in the background of international economic relations, justifies us in exploring hopefully the possibilities of new techniques which may help us to realize the wider objectives to which public opinion now increasingly attaches importance. We should not be wasting our time if we took the trouble to form in our minds some picture of the world economic conditions which would suit us best, and which would serve as a useful standard of reference by which we might judge the actual realities, and of the institutional framework which might facilitate an approximation as close as possible to these conditions.

SAFEGUARDS AGAINST STRUCTURAL CHANGES

Technological changes in other countries may sometimes be embarrassing to us, especially if they are on a large scale, or if we are obliged to adjust ourselves to their consequences very suddenly. Nevertheless, the most that we should endeavour to do, even in an ideal world, would be to ensure that they occurred in the most orderly possible way, and as this is almost certainly beyond our power, our wisest course is probably just to accept them as they come. There are so many directions in which we anticipate, with some confidence, that technological changes will be advantageous to us, that it would be absurd to think of trying to prevent other people from making their own experiments in this field. The frailties of human nature may make it difficult for us to maintain an austere objectivity in comparing the consequences of technological changes which are favourable to us, and of which therefore we approve, with the consequences whose first impact may be unfavourable and therefore disliked by us, but clearly in this matter we cannot expect to be allowed to pick and choose.

On any hypothesis, it is an interest of the first order of importance for Great Britain to maintain its own productive efficiency at the highest possible level, and few post-war reconstruction programmes fail to include some reference to the more efficient organization of scientific research which ought to prove an important instrument for this purpose. Any large-scale improvements in our own efficiency are, however, likely to be just as embarrassing for other economies as improvements in the efficiency of others may be for us; in an ideal world order, we might hope to find national policies generally more appreciative of the wisdom of flexibility in production structures, for such flexibility would diminish the embarrassments arising from the impact of competition from our own more efficiently produced exports. We might go further and speculate about the possibility that the more powerful economies, where technological improvements are most likely to originate, might recognize some responsibility for easing the adaptations which weaker economies may find it impossible to face if left entirely dependent upon their own resources. Some Americans have, for example, already asserted that the future of synthetic rubber is not something to be determined exclusively by reference to comparative monetary costs. The necessity for finding some alternative method of earning a livelihood in Malaya and the Netherlands East Indies must also, they assert, be taken into account. Equally, the fostering of beet sugar production in Great Britain places upon the British people a special responsibility for the welfare of the West India islands, which, as a result of past history, have now come to rely exclusively upon sugar production as the foundation of their economic life. How far views of this kind will find any practical expression is still doubtful, but it would clearly be an advance of major import-ance if more careful account were everywhere taken of the indirect costs, both internal and international, of technological changes, and even modest steps initiated to assist its innocent victims in other countries to find the new place in the structure of production which it would be in the general interest for them to occupy.

To submit to the inconveniences imposed by technological change in other countries is one thing; many, however, would think that to give positive assistance to the process was some-thing entirely different, and there has often been a strong feeling in favour of at least a negative attitude towards, for example, the further industrialization of the less highly deve-loped economies. Why, it is asked, should we actively promote the growth of new industries in countries which have formerly provided good markets for our exports, and thereby make certain a decline in some of our industries which otherwise might remain merely an unpleasant possibility? There is a long history of obstruction motivated by considerations such as this. Until well into the nineteenth century, Great Britain attempted to prevent the emigration of machinery and artisans, fearing lest the arts of manufacture should thereby be promoted in other countries, and at a much later date Brazil was still attempting to prohibit the export of rubber plants from which subsequently emerged a competition that was highly embarrass-ing to the Brazilian economy. Formal action of this kind is now less common than it was, but the ideas upon which it was based are still not without influence. Past obstructions have, no doubt, sometimes distorted the normal course of economic development, but, on the whole, they have failed to provide the protection at which they aimed. Sooner or later, the changes which it was hoped to prevent have usually been made, and early attempts at obstruction may even have made the adjust-ments which subsequently became necessary more difficult than they need have been. The capacity of any single economy to hamper industrialization elsewhere, whose immediate effects may be embarrassing to itself, is in any event strictly limited. If, moreover, Great Britain has any permanent competitive advantages in international trade, they lie predominantly in the production of goods within the range of purchasing power of people with relatively high income. A wisely directed policy of industrialization ought to increase the number of these people, and as in any event obstruction would probably be unsuccessful, except perhaps in a very short run, and would certainly provoke suspicion and resentment, it would appear to be a sound long-run British interest to refrain from any attempt to obstruct changes in other economies which would tend to increase the number of people who can afford to buy British exports.

The effects of spontaneous changes in foreign consumers' demands lie even more obviously outside the range of our control. Some bilateralist proposals, indeed, imply that foreign customers might be compelled or induced to purchase British goods, despite their preferences for goods of a different origin. The ideas lying behind these suggestions will be more conveniently examined in our subsequent discussion of the alternatives to an open international system, but on the face of it they do not offer a very promising foundation for a permanent or stable policy. Concrete plans for pushing British exports after the war also often give a prominent place to salesmanship and advertising, designed to mould consumers' demand in the pattern most convenient to ourselves. We cannot afford to be entirely indifferent to these activities, but even if we rate their value very high, their importance as a stabilizing factor remains quite slight.

POLICY DECISIONS OF OTHER GOVERNMENTS

The organization of safeguards against the risks of instability arising from the policy decisions of the governments of other states has both deserved and received much more serious attention. Either by the ratification of a treaty, or in association with a continuously operating international institution—and these two techniques are clearly not inconsistent with each other—governments might be induced to renounce certain practices which directly or indirectly threatened to damage our employment situation. Leaving aside for the moment the problem of seeking for formal commitments for the maintenance of adequate internal employment levels, there are several other directions in which formal international safeguards of this kind might have great value. So long as other states preserve and, from time to time, exercise their right to use their own unfettered discretion in relation to tariff levels, the imposition or administration of foreign exchange controls, or the determination of the value of their national currency, we are constantly liable to incalculable unemployment risks. If other governments can be persuaded to qualify their rights in these matters, perhaps to accept beforehand certain principles for the guidance of their conduct, or to agree to make such changes as from time to time they may consider necessary only after consultation with an appropriately constituted international organ, the benefits in the way of stability which we should thus be able to enjoy would be well worth the "sacrifice" implied in the acceptance by our own government of the same limitation upon its own right to do precisely as it pleased.

Where the relevant influences are so closely interrelated, it is not easy, and perhaps not very meaningful, to attempt any precise measurement of the contributions made by each one of them to such instability as may be inflicted upon our economy from outside. The right of other nations suddenly to impose quotas, exchange controls, etc. may, however, give shocks to our exporting industries quite as severe as any likely to arise from a contraction of demand in conditions of depression. By participating in an international system which limited that right, we might gain as much on the security and stability side as we lost by being exposed to a wider range of external fluctuations.

In relation to these and other closely related problems, the approach which has now become most fashionable contemplates the formulation of general rules to be applied to all national economies. There is much to be said for this technique. Nevertheless, it might be doubted whether more satisfactory results would not sometimes be obtained, and obtained more quickly, from an approach which at first sight appeared more modest. It would be both unfair and injudicious to attempt to place the whole responsibility for the future economic development of the world upon the United States, unique though the importance of that country's economy may be. Nevertheless, there are quite clear-cut distinctions to be drawn between the attention rightly paid to the effects upon their neighbours of the policy decisions of the more powerful economies, and the comparative indifference with which the vagaries and idiosyncrasies of the weaker economies could safely be regarded. In principle, there is not a single country whose currency policy, for example, is a matter of purely domestic concern, but in fact, the inconveniences caused elsewhere by short-sighted decisions on the part, say, of Paraguay or of Siam, would be so slight as compared with the effects of sharp divergences of policy between any of the more powerful economies that they might well be left entirely out of account in the thinking of practical statesmen. An effective understanding between the more important economies might, even if it lacked a binding constitutional form, be a target much more worthy of intense effort than a more formal document which endeavoured to take into account the peculiar circumstances of all economies, however they might be situated.

In the nature of things, formal safeguards are scarcely conceivable against the risks of instability arising from a permanent decline in the level of income of our customers abroad. We can merely do our best to ensure that, so far as it depends on us, the fundamental conditions for their prosperity shall not be impaired, and while our responsibility in this connection may sometimes be quite far-reaching, it is necessarily also always limited, and cannot easily be expressed beforehand in terms of any formal obligations. The restoration of economies which are on the downgrade usually demands some radical structural adjustments on their part, and we must be careful not to place unnecessary obstructions in their way. The problem is essentially the same as that of the economic development of backward or depressed areas. It has often been argued that the adjustments needed in such cases are so drastic that it is hopeless to expect them to emerge in response to the automatic mechanism of an open international system. There is no doubt often a strong case in such circumstances for special emergency measures, but while it is true that a weak economy struggling to find its feet in a new situation may often be peculiarly exposed to the risks of ruthless competition from stronger economies who have already established their position in world markets, it should not be forgotten that the machinery of international control can also easily be used to retard the growth of weaker economies. The equality of opportunity which it is the purpose of an open international system to ensure, however imperfect its practice may often have been, is a direct interest of those who have still their way to make in the world.

SAFEGUARDS AGAINST CYCLICAL FLUCTUATIONS

Some readers may be a little impatient with the attention which we have so far given to causes of employment instability other than those which arise from cyclical fluctuations in the incomes of other economies, for in the current discussions of British post-war international commitments it is the latter problem which has so far almost monopolized attention. Its importance cannot, of course, be questioned, but it is precisely because there is already a high degree of awareness of this fact, that it is proper here to place a little more emphasis upon other and no less important aspects of the post-war British situation which otherwise might easily be neglected.

As has already been suggested, it is often extremely difficult at the time to distinguish between the effects of cyclical fluctuations and those of more deep-seated disequilibria in either our economic structure or the economic structure of other countries. There is no reason to suppose that the acuteness of this difficulty will diminish in the immediate future, and we should be careful lest elaborate preparations against the risks of cyclical fluctuations should induce a dangerous neglect of the other factors which no less urgently demand attention. The long-run structural adjustments to which we have frequently referred are by their nature unlikely to present themselves to the public as problems calling for prompt and urgent attention. But this makes it all the more necessary that they should at no time be overlooked. For the crises in which the failure to make necessary adjustments culminates are usually the conclusion of a long process of development, and the fact that the real significance of the symptoms is so easily misunderstood in the early stages of this process is one important reason why the crises are sometimes so difficult to handle. The better prepared we are to deal without delay with the problems of structural adjustment presented by fundamental changes in the international conditions of supply and demand, the less numerous would be the occasions when we were called upon to offset the effects of cyclical fluctuations and the less violent the fluctuations which we should have to try to counter.

At least one aspect, though not the most important, of the problem of cyclical fluctuations has indeed already been touched upon, for the pressure to adopt a policy of competitive exchange depreciation is most likely to make itself felt when cyclical fluctuations are troublesome. Few economies would wantonly depreciate their exchange rates unless they were already in a difficult situation, and the pressure of cyclical depression is an important, though not the only, disability which would make this policy seem attractive.

This, however, at best does not by itself carry us very far. The right to depreciate our exchange rate in suitable circumstances without laying ourselves open to the charge of international anti-social conduct, merely provides us with an instrument to be kept in reserve in case things go wrong. The more important question is whether we can get any assurances that other economies will not behave in such a way as to compel a resort to this instrument.

THE AUSTRALIAN PROPOSALS

The possibility of assurances of this kind has been widely canvassed, the view being sometimes defended that unless such assurances are forthcoming we should decline to face the risks of membership of an open international economic system. The question may most conveniently be examined by taking as a text the most elaborate proposition of this kind which has so far received official support, though, as we shall see, its sponsors felt obliged, no doubt for reasons to which our attention will be directed below, to put forward their proposals in terms much less definite and precise than some of the unofficial speculations in the same field have suggested.

The Australian Government has been the most active in pressing for international agreement along these lines, and their views can be conveniently studied in the terms of the draft resolution upon the subject submitted to the International Labour Conference at Philadelphia in April 1944 by Mr J. A. Beasley, the Australian Minister for Supply and Shipping.[1] The resolution was ultimately rejected in committee by 12 Government and 5 Employer votes, against 3 Government, 1 Employer, and 6 Workers.

The undertaking to which the Australian Government proposed that signatories should subscribe would have bound each of them to undertake "a national obligation to its own people and an international obligation to the other signatory Governments, henceforth to take such measures as may be necessary and practicable" to permit the attainment of a high level of employment among its people, an end recognized as "not only fundamental to their material well-being", but as also contributing "through the channels of trade to the creation of employment for the peoples of other countries and to an increase in their well-being". Such an obligation, indeed, falls far short of a detailed prescription for national policy, but in addition to an agreement for the collection of more satisfactory statistics of national employment and unemployment, the regular submission of such statistics to other Governments, through the International Labour Organization, at intervals not exceeding three months, the presentation of reports by each Government "on the state of employment of its people and on the economic policies which have been used or are contemplated to combat unemployment", and participation in

[1] Record of Proceedings, International Labour Conference, Twenty-sixth Session, Philadelphia, 1944, pp. 339-341.

conferences to be summoned if, in the opinion of the International Labour Organization, "a serious decline in employment is developing in any of the signatory countries (for causes whether avoidable or unavoidable by the Governments of the countries concerned), for the purpose of examining and reporting upon possible national and international measures to restore the level of employment and to prevent the spread of unemployment to other countries", each Government was also to be asked in the event of a serious decline in the level of the employment of its people, to undertake "to consider measures to restore the level of employment such as: (a) stimulation of private investment; (b) increase in public investment; (c) increased consumption expenditure; (d) expansion of overseas investment where appropriate."

These proposals were all carefully set out in terms which did not infringe the principle of national sovereignty, as that term is often popularly understood. Governments were merely asked to undertake to "consider" measures; they were not to be formally obliged to put them into operation. It was, however, clearly contemplated that if they failed to do so, other governments should then be entitled to regard themselves as freed from some at least of the parallel international obligations which they might have assumed in other policy fields. The relation, as interpreted by the Australian Government, between obligations in regard to employment policy, and obligations implied in the reconstruction of an open international system was clearly expressed by Mr Beasley in the following words: "Without an employment agreement, other international economic proposals will be no more than a dangerously deceptive veneer, simply covering the fundamental problems of international society. For many countries, an employment agreement would, perhaps, be an essential precondition of other economic and political agreements. Countries cannot accept the implications of monetary, commercial or commodity schemes, without knowing far more about the domestic policies of others . . . An assurance regarding the kind of domestic policy which countries will follow, embodied in a formal employment agreement, will facilitate very greatly the successful negotiation of international agreement on other aspects of international economic collaboration."[1] "If the United States is unwilling to undertake some employment obligations, we must hesitate before entering into discussions on other aspects of international economic collaboration, and we could not feel obliged to undertake any commitments which limited our freedom of action to protect our economy against depressed conditions overseas."

It is, however, clearly asking for a good deal to suggest the ready acceptance of a procedure for regularizing a formal international inquest upon the domestic policies of certain countries, whenever in the view of the International Labour Organization they threatened the stability of employment elsewhere, and to make recommendations for a revision of these policies. In principle, there is nothing to be said against action of this kind, and any trend in this direction should be welcomed and encouraged, but it is doubtful whether many governments have yet reached the stage where they could be counted upon to give it their whole-hearted support.

The resolution was also open to the criticism that the techniques which it selected for formal approval were too narrowly conceived. The resolution ultimately adopted by the Conference on this subject urged "that all practicable measures should be taken to maintain a high and steady level of employment, to minimize fluctuations in business activity, and to assure a steadily expanding volume of production". The means recommended for this purpose were not, however, confined to "fiscal, monetary and other measures, including useful public works, to sustain the volume of demand for goods and services at a high level, while avoiding the dangers of an inflationary spiral of prices and wages", a group of activities in which "an adequate income security system" also found a place. The list also included "measures to discourage monopolistic practices and to encourage technological progress, to maintain a reasonably flexible system of prices and wages, to encourage transfers of workers and productive resources from declining to expanding industries, and to attain a high degree of mobility of

[1] Op. cit., p. 33.

resources and freedom of access to alternative employments; . . . the adjustment of tax systems, removal of artificial barriers limiting access to resources and markets, the relaxation of unreasonable restrictions imposed by governmental agencies or by business or by labour organizations, and the maintenance of a high and stable demand for goods; and the provision of improved and more generally accessible educational and training facilities".[1] All these have some relevance, and some of them have a very direct relevance, to the long-term problem of maintaining simultaneously high levels of employment and high standards of living, but the difficulties of the task of formulating binding international conventions which would do justice to each one of them in its intricate interrelations with all the others, would clearly be formidable.

To press for "safeguards" which so intimately concern the internal policies of other countries is clearly a matter of unusual delicacy, and especially when we are thinking of measures for the control of employment, we should be wise to interpret the word "safeguard" in the widest possible sense. The existence of formal agreements or written undertakings does not invariably or necessarily justify any increase in our confidence about the future, and the alternatives which we might appropriately consider run all the way from an entirely informal or implicit understanding, based upon past experience of the attitudes which we could take for granted that other economies would adopt, to a rigid and elaborate international agreement prescribing in detail the policies which all the parties to the agreement were under an obligation to apply, and providing machinery for reviewing what they actually did and applying effective pressure to ensure that any neglect of their responsibilities was quickly remedied. In the post-war world, there is indeed scarcely the slightest possibility that we shall have any experience of either of these two theoretical possibilities. There has, as yet, been no time to get experience of what other economies can be relied upon to do in the new conditions into which we are now moving, and our recollection of the fluctuations of the last thirty years is still so vivid that there will

[1] Op. cit., pp. 336-7.

certainly be widespread reluctance merely to trust to the wisdom of the spontaneous decisions of others. We should, however, not forget that in many spheres of human activity, the supports upon which we can most confidently rely are often never embodied in any formal document of any kind. Starting afresh, as we are now obliged to do, after a sharp break in the normal continuity of human history, we naturally seek for something a little more precise and definite. In the long run, however, the foundations of our economic system may be less firmly based, the more strongly we feel obliged to insist upon the assumption of formal obligations. Our own attitude towards proposals to accept formal obligations often provides a vivid illustration of the still strong reluctance of sovereign states to abandon their "freedom" to make their own decisions on matters of high policy in the light of their own judgment at the time of what will suit their interests best. We may, if we like, insist upon the short-sightedness of this prejudice, but it would be over-optimistic to expect that its influence will not still be considerable in the immediate future, and we should there-fore do well to resign ourselves to the necessity of making do with assurances much less precise than we might like to have.

Those who press most strongly for international agreement to guarantee employment levels often claim this as an essential prior condition for international economic collaboration in other directions. As we have already suggested, it is doubtful whether such problems are most profitably approached in terms of rather rigid priorities. What in fact we really need is effective simultaneous action along a number of fronts. Our doubts are further strengthened when we reflect that in this particular context, if there is to be any indubitable priority, it is without any doubt intended to be reserved for the domestic policy of a single country, the United States, however diplo-matically this fact may be wrapped up in phraseology about a general international agreement. From the lesson which past experience has often given us, that formal obligations may be of much less significance than what people actually do, the conclusion should perhaps be drawn that the future might work out rather better from our point of view if we refrained from pressing too hard for formal commitments.[1]

In any event, in urging other economies to follow the example which we propose to set, we should bear in mind that our own policy is still in large measure experimental. Even if it could be demonstrated without a shadow of doubt that it would certainly give us the degree of success claimed for it, the conditions of other economies might differ so significantly from ours that they would be quite justified in doubting whether similar results would follow from its application to themselves. We might more convincingly urge other economies to follow our example, if we could already point to concrete results which our own policy had achieved. But for the most part, this must for some time remain a matter for the future, and we cannot reasonably complain if people in other countries prefer to suspend judgment, especially if they take a view different from ours, either of the wisdom of relying upon forces, which, if uncontrolled, would keep prices moving steadily upwards, or of the effectiveness of the machinery likely to be available to keep price movements in check. At least we should be careful not to appear to be pressing our policy upon the attention of others, by methods and in terms uncomfortably similar to those of the vendor of a new patent medicine for which no convincing record of "cures" can yet be claimed.

THE BRITISH TRANSITIONAL PROBLEM

For purposes both of analysis and of exposition it is legitimate to differentiate rather sharply between the problems of long-term policy and those of the immediate post-war

---

[1] If formal international commitments are to be taken seriously, the most careful consideration must be given to the definition and measurement of full employment. For if, in the event of some other economy having failed to maintain a proper level of employment, we are to be absolved from the obligation to observe some of the undertakings which limit the freedom of, for example, our commercial policy, the gravest embarrassments will result if we have no objective tests which will make it quite clear to every one concerned that a situation justifying this absolution has arisen. This point should be borne in mind by any one disposed to be impatient at what he might hastily regard as our rather elaborate discussion of the concept of full employment, in an earlier section.

transitional period. The practical statesman is, however, seldom in a position where he can safely press this distinction very far. The two sets of problems must be dealt with at the same time, and in considering the kind of world in which he is being invited to live, the British statesman in particular must bear in mind the repercussions of his decisions upon his immediate transitional problems, as well as upon the prospects of success for a long-run employment programme. In existing circumstances, it is indeed not a matter for surprise that the greater part of the current discussion of our problems has centred, not around the interrelation of full employment policy and international economic policy, but rather upon the impact of the obligations of Article VII of the Mutual Aid Agreement upon the readjustments which Great Britain is obliged to face during the transitional period into which we have now entered.

The peculiar difficulties which Great Britain will have to encounter in the transitional period are now in general outline fairly well known, and it is not necessary here to elaborate them in detail, except perhaps to remind ourselves that they may not be quite so peculiar as we are sometimes inclined to think, being indeed, in one form or another, common to many economies throughout the world. As a result of the transfer to other owners of a large part of the overseas assets, the income from which formerly financed a substantial fraction of our normal import trade, and of the accumulation of war debts in a variety of forms, the British post-war balance of payments will be in a sadly disordered condition, and it will be necessary to take special care to ensure that it is not thrown further out of gear by indiscriminate importing. The problem is, however, not only peculiarly difficult: it is also unusually delicate. In the course of its development, the economy of the United Kingdom has moved into a position of dependence upon imports which is peculiar, if not unique, and from which it may now be next to impossible to withdraw. There are other economies for whom imports provide a larger fraction of their aggregate consumption than for the United Kingdom, but the fraction of the British real national income which is supplied by imports probably includes a larger proportion than any other of goods which, if even modest standards of living are to be maintained, must be given a high priority. To use a popular phrase, an unusually large proportion of British imports are essential goods, and though in our use of the word "essential" we often forget that, if we are obliged to, we can get along without a great many of the things to which we have become accustomed, the margin of luxury or near-luxury goods in our imports which might be sacrificed without much inconvenience is certainly quite small. It is an awkward consequence of this traditional structure of British imports, that it is only with some difficulty that a frank exposition of the post-war situation avoids the appearance of a rather unconvincing plea that the rest of the world owes a duty to the people of this country to restore their standard of living to a level not very different from that enjoyed before the war. It is, indeed, important that the international implications of Britain's post-war economic difficulties should be widely appreciated elsewhere, and there is evidence that already they are receiving serious attention. A detailed examination of the most appropriate methods for filling the threatened gap in the British balance of payments lies outside the scope of the present study, but as some of them are also relevant to the general issues with which we are concerned, a few comments may be permissible.

It is now a commonplace to say that, if British standards of living are not to deteriorate unduly, and if the British economy is to achieve something like assured stability in the post-war world, the volume of British exports must be increased by at least 50 per cent as compared with the pre-war level. The basis for this somewhat specious statistical precision is not always very closely defined—and the tendency in recent months has been to raise the target to a still higher figure— but there is no doubt whatever that a very large expansion of British exports is highly desirable, and no one need fear that a 50 per cent increase, if we could get it, would turn out to be embarrassingly large. But if this increase has to be sought within a framework of international economic relations as cramped as that which threatened to crystallize during the years immediately preceding the outbreak of war, the prospects of success are not at all bright. The task will be difficult enough even in favourable circumstances, but in an expanding world economy, where, even if our relative share of the cake was smaller than it used to be, we should at least have a fighting chance of getting an adequate slice from an expanding cake, it should not be quite impossible. For the attainment of this end, the same flexibility of economic structure, which, we have already insisted, has much more importance for the maintenance of full employment than some popular discussions would suggest, is generally recognized as of first-rate importance. Both in the long and in the short run, the most hopeful method for finding assured outlets for a greatly expanded British export trade is the encouragement of the most efficient methods of production capable of turning out things of a kind and at a price which will be attractive to our customers abroad.

Whatever success we may hope to achieve along this line in the immediate future, there is no undue pessimism implied in the fear that it may not by itself be adequate to solve the British problem with the speed which we should like. Far-sighted observers in other countries have had no difficulty in agreeing that it would be very much against their own interests to leave the British economy to find its own way out of the difficulties created by the inevitable accumulation of over-whelming wartime obligations. Already before the matter had been brought to a head by the Washington negotiations, provisionally concluded by the Financial Agreement of December 6, 1945, the view had been expressed in the United States that the special difficulties of Great Britain should be dealt with before any one was asked to undertake the far-reaching long-term obligations involved in membership of the Bretton Woods International Monetary Fund and of the International Bank for Reconstruction and Development. "The 12 billion accumulation of sterling war balances in London", it was said, "is not dissimilar in nature or in magnitude from the Inter-Allied debt or the Reparations problem that be-devilled international relations during the inter-war period. That England should have to bear it alone, is just as questionable from the standpoint of equity as was the Inter-Allied debt."[1]

The natural course for any one in temporary financial difficulties, who has a reasonable prospect of ultimate recovery, is to negotiate a credit or loan on terms as favourable as possible in some quarter which is financially strong enough to make the advance that is needed. In the case of Great Britain, the obvious course from which such financial support could be drawn is the United States. There has been some reluctance in Great Britain, natural enough in view of the large volume of existing indebtedness, which in any case presents us with a series of highly embarrassing problems, to contemplate seriously action of this kind. There is a natural pride which finds it difficult to realize that an economy with a long and honourable history as an international creditor should now have reached a position where the relations hitherto regarded as "normal" might appropriately be reversed. But while pride is a factor which cannot safely be ignored in applied economics, there seem to be no good reasons for allowing it to determine our judgment in relation to matters of such first-rate importance.

Even if, however, we were prepared to pocket our pride in this connection, we should still prudently inquire whether the acceptance of such credits, on however favourable terms, might not mean merely a dangerous delay in facing up to the real facts of the changed situation. In recent years, the world has had so much unhappy experience of the difficulties of servicing large foreign debts in circumstances where national commercial policies had not been properly adjusted to new creditor-debtor relationships, that a prudent statesman now naturally hesitates before he commits his country to any serious risk of the repetition of these difficulties. A solution which is not to be merely a temporary stop-gap must embrace far-reaching agreement on commercial policy as well, and it is equally clear, though perhaps not yet so generally understood, that the trade adjustments which ought logically to follow any radical

---

[1] J. H. Williams: "International Monetary Plans after Bretton Woods", *Foreign Affairs*, October 1944, p. 21.

shift in the traditional balance of international payments inevitably include equally radical shifts in the comparative height of the tariff levels of the different countries concerned. And even if a debtor were not anxious to insist on adequate assurances in regard to these matters, it is scarcely conceivable that international credits on the scale now proposed should be either forthcoming or accepted without some general understanding in regard to most of the issues with which our study has been concerned. In the proposals which were announced at the end of 1945 there is a clear recognition of these facts, though not necessarily so clear as many people would like, and the further elaboration of our argument on these points will therefore be more conveniently undertaken in the next section, when we pass from the discussion of safeguards in general to the discussion of the safeguards which actually have been or are likely to be offered.

A GUARANTEED GLOBAL IMPORT DEMAND

There is, however, at least theoretically conceivable a "safeguard" of another type which properly calls for examination here. Balances of payments generally would be protected and the risks of unemployment at least substantially diminished, if each of the more important economies were to guarantee that its aggregate demand for imports in general would not be allowed to fall below some agreed and specified level. Is it quite inconceivable that some such guarantee might be given? Some of the members of the school which strongly approves the official Australian approach to these problems have gone so far as to suggest that we should demand "an explicit provision that, if some nation fails to maintain full employment and its unemployment figures exceed some agreed percentage, the others should be free to protect themselves against further shrinkage of trade by developing compensatory trade among themselves."[1] Whether the political and administrative difficulties of such a proposal are so great as to make it one of merely academic interest is a matter on which there are naturally sharp differences of opinion, but even those who take a

[1] Nicholas Kaldor: *Manchester Guardian*, December 12, 1945.

hopeful view of it might wisely consider whether the same end might not be reached, with less risk of provoking resentful opposition, by pressing for the administratively much simpler device of the guarantee of an adequate global import demand.

The implications of this proposal may be made a little clearer by a comparison with some of the internal conditions most favourable to stability of employment. Without prejudging any of the specific devices proposed for the purpose, there is clearly a strong *prima facie* case for maintaining, by suitable methods, as stable a general level of internal demand as we can. Such general stability would, however, as has often been pointed out, be compatible with violent fluctuations in the demand for particular things, and therefore also in employment, and we have already seen how some writers on full employment have proposed to meet this difficulty by supplementary devices designed to stabilize demand in selected sectors of the economy. Objections of various kinds can legitimately be raised against these supplementary devices; whether or not these objections should be pushed so far as to demand a complete abandonment of this approach to the problem, we have argued that the urgency of the difficulties which it is designed to meet will be greatly diminished if we take care to maintain the highest possible degree of flexibility within our economy, so that productive resources can, when necessary, be shifted quickly.

However we may think it proper to treat the general internal level of demand in our own economy, there still remains the possibility of fluctuations in demand arising outside. And whether or not responsibility for maintaining internal demand can properly be assigned to some central authority, no comparable authority either exists or is likely to exist which could make its influence felt throughout the whole of the world economy in such a way as to ensure that the general level of demand for imports should not be allowed to fall. Any action taken with this end in view would have to be the responsibility of individual national governments, so that nothing but a piecemeal approach to this problem is possible. For practical purposes, however, the number of governments important for this purpose is quite small. If their demand were adequately maintained, the demand from the smaller economies would be unlikely to cause any trouble, so that a piecemeal approach might still give sufficiently satisfactory results.

Bilateralist and regionalist programmes for international trade, in effect, propose to meet this difficulty by securing for the British economy an assurance of an adequate demand for British exports by tying other economies to the purchase of more or less clearly defined quantities of British goods. There are serious objections in principle to this approach, and we shall suggest later that there are even more serious practical grounds for rejecting it as inadequate for British post-war needs. But instead of asking for the assurances for the particular export trades of particular countries which are implied in these programmes, we might quite rationally ask each of the main economies to guarantee that its aggregate demand for imports, from whatever source, would not be allowed to fall below a certain agreed level. The idea of tying down import demand for the benefit of particular exporting countries is thus entirely rejected, but the general level of international demand for the goods which enter into international trade would be maintained by the guarantee of a global import quota from the more important trading countries.

It would be an incidental advantage of an arrangement of this kind, that it would leave a wide measure of freedom to each country to determine, according to its own convenience, the methods for carrying on its international trade, and in particular, to select whatever means it thought proper for bringing imports up to the guaranteed level if for any reason they threatened, if left to themselves, to fall below it. The less any single country need be asked to bind itself to specific detailed action the better, provided that the main objective is attained, and this condition would be adequately satisfied under the arrangements here outlined. The elaboration of general principles of conduct for international trade policy has always been a matter of special difficulty when the parties most directly concerned had adopted radically different foundations for their economic activity, and indeed, such attention as has already been given to the principle of a global import quota has, for the most part, had its origin directly in the desire to evade these difficulties. But even if trade were everywhere to be conducted according to the same principles, the obligation, by one means or another to be determined according to one's own discretion, to check any tendency for imports in general to fall below some agreed level, would be a powerful stabilizing influence.

126

Chapter IX

WHAT SAFEGUARDS ARE LIKELY
TO BE OFFERED?

T HE next stage in our argument requires an examination of
such "safeguards" as at present appear to lie within the
range of practical politics. We shall begin with measures which
might be taken on their own initiative by other countries to
stabilize their own economies, and which incidentally would
thus afford us some protection against the risk of their instabi-
lities being transmitted to ourselves, and follow this up with
an examination of international measures, strictly so called.

IMPORTANCE OF UNITED STATES POLICY

There is no part of the world where influences might not be
generated whose impact would have important consequences
for the stability of the British economy, and in an exhaustive
survey there is scarcely a single area which, from this point of
view, we could afford to neglect. The impact from some areas
indeed might accurately be described as a repercussion from
decisions originally made in Great Britain itself, for there are
still many parts of the world for whom the decisions most
significant for economic policy come from this country. No
survey which can pretend to completeness is possible here, and
in any event, the policy of the United States is generally agreed
to be of such first-rate importance for the whole of the rest of
the world, that we are justified in concentrating our attention
upon that country.

Some of the reasons why United States policy deserves this
special attention have already been mentioned. The very
large share of the United States both in world production and
in world trade, and in particular in trade in some of the basic
raw materials, make it inevitable that the ups and downs in
United States economic activity should have immediate repercussions nearly everywhere else. But United States policy is
also, in a peculiar degree, autonomous. Its makers cannot

ignore events in other parts of the world, but more often than not the initiative rests with them. And either because the fundamental causes of the trade cycle, by their nature, operate most directly within the United States economy, or on account of some peculiar temperamental characteristics of the American people, it appears to be more susceptible than most to violent fluctuations, so that any failure to keep these fluctuations under control has far-reaching consequences. Whether fairly or not, the United States has, in the minds of many people, acquired a bad reputation on account of the risks which any country closely associated with it appears to run of having to submit to violent economic upheavals, in the initiation of which it is widely felt that other countries have played little or no significant part. Just how far this belief is strictly justified, we need not here pause to inquire. When things go wrong, there is a natural eagerness on the part of all concerned to put as much as possible of the blame on to the other fellow, and it need, therefore, occasion little surprise if many in the United States insist that "the explicit or implicit assumption that the severity of world depression of the thirties was due almost entirely to the instability of the American economy and economic mismanagement in the United States is greatly exaggerated . . . . There are plenty of cases in which foreign countries managed to produce their own depressions without American help."[1] But even if a good deal of exaggeration is admitted to be highly probable, a sober analysis would certainly give a high priority in any list of the significant causes of the economic disorders of our generation to the errors, both of commission and of omission, of United States policy during the nineteen-twenties and nineteen-thirties, though it would equally certainly insist that, within the limits of their power and resources, other economies had also made significant contributions to the general confusion.[2] Can we have any guarantee, the question then naturally arises, that those errors will not be repeated?

[1] G. Haberler in *Economic Reconstruction*, ed. Seymour Harris, New York, McGraw Hill, 1945, pp. 322n, 329.
[2] In view of the emphatic insistence in Australia, to which we have already referred, upon the overwhelming international importance of national full employment policies, it is perhaps significant that it is also an Australian

There is certainly no doubt about the reality of current fears of future trends in United States policy. Sometimes the dominant fear is one of uncontrolled inflation. Wartime expenditure has everywhere created a potentially inflationary situation, whose control will test to the utmost the resolution and skill of national monetary authorities. Will the United States, with its deeply rooted prejudices against price and other controls of a similar kind, succeed in preventing this situation from getting out of hand, and thereby rendering ineffective the well-designed stabilizing intentions of other countries? At other times, and especially among those who retain vivid recollections of the Great Depression, the picture which arouses alarm is that of other economies compelled by their association with the United States to submit to a catastrophic deflation which, if this association did not exist, might have been avoided, and even, as some confident people would argue, easily avoided. In general, the economic history of the United States is widely interpreted, both in that country and elsewhere, as proof of a peculiar susceptibility to the fluctuations of the trade cycle, and many people in other countries who believe that they have discovered a cure for this disease which, provided it was not contracted in too virulent a form, they could apply with every hope of success, fear that contact with the United States may subject them to infection of such a malignant kind that the cure will be ineffective.

---

writer who has recently thought it worth while to remind us not only that "Great responsibility attaches to the leaders of the American economy to provide the basis on which these ideals (i.e. high employment, a rising standard of living, and an expanding world economy) can be progressively realized", but also that "An equal responsibility rests with the less favoured countries whose economic power has been impaired by the war to pursue a policy which will maintain maximum co-operation with the United States." (D. B. Copland, *Report on Economic Conditions in the United Kingdom, United States of America, and Canada*, p. 6.) Referring to the insistence in 1925 upon restoring the pre-war external value of sterling, another American writer, who is by no means sparing in his criticisms of United States policy, adds the comment that "until these things are forgotten and until England is prepared to eschew over-valuation, her spokesmen might more humbly pursue international monetary co-operation, and not assume that English finance, past and future, affords a form by which other nations may be judged as eligible for, or exempt from, quarantine." (H. C. Simons, *Journal of Political Economy*, September 1945, p. 224.)

At the present time, there is naturally a great deal of anxious speculation everywhere about probable employment trends during the next few years. A great deal has been written on the subject in the United States, and interest in those aspects of the problem which are peculiar to that country is, in the circumstances which we have described, scarcely less lively elsewhere. The minds of most of us would be a good deal easier if we could discover exactly what was going to happen to employment in the United States during the next five years. In the nature of things, this knowledge is necessarily withheld from us, but practical statesmen who have somehow or other to adjust themselves to events beyond their control are quite justified in forming the best guess they can, inevitably based though it must be on highly imperfect knowledge. Sometimes the issue is presented in the form of the question, will the United States succeed in attaining and maintaining full employment? This is a legitimate enough preoccupation for Americans themselves, but as has already been argued, people elsewhere may be asking for a good deal more than is necessary from the standpoint of their own comfort if they insist upon full employment, as sometimes interpreted, in the United States as an essential condition to justify the intimate contacts with the American economy implied in the re-establishment of a new multilateral international economic system. It is no doubt desirable on other grounds that the highest possible level of stable employment should be maintained in the United States, but the practical consequences for us of the differences between this level and one somewhat lower or less stable might not be very important, so that we should do well to be content with an examination of the more modest question, what are the chances of the United States maintaining a satisfactorily stable level of economic activity?

Statistical estimates of national income have been widely used in discussing both these questions, the attempt being made to determine the level below which the national money income of the United States must not be allowed to fall, if an intractable unemployment situation is not to develop, or to predict the level which, on certain hypotheses, is likely to be

130

reached. Investigators are, however, by no means agreed as to the figure which may most usefully be used for either of these purposes, though some of the disputes which the estimates have provoked are due to little more than differences of opinion about the most appropriate statistical technique. According to one writer, "the nation will need to produce a gross national product of about $200 billion in 1944 prices, in order to maintain 'full' employment in the post-war period",[1] or a national income of about $160 billion, and it was estimated that "private capital formation plus government expenditure on goods and services, will need to be between $71 and $87 billion in order to maintain full employment" at this level of income. Another estimate, that of the Brookings Institute, placing greater emphasis on post-war contractions of the labour force and disregarding historical trends in productivity, arrived at a much lower estimate for national income, $123 billion.

It is impossible, within the limits of this study, to pretend to be able to offer any useful critical analysis of these and similar estimates.[2] Useful though they may be, they are necessarily highly speculative, and their significance for our purposes is, in any event, much diminished if it is agreed that the risks of the British economy being infected by American instability might be reduced to manageable proportions by something less than the attainment of full employment in the United States.

In the nature of things, it is unlikely that we can have any certainty in our guesses about the general attitude likely to be adopted in the United States towards the maintenance of high levels of employment. The United States is a democratic country in which policy may change from time to time in accordance with the swings of public opinion which are a natural and proper characteristic of a democracy. There are sharp differences of opinion there on nearly every fundamental economic issue, and these differences are frequently expressed with an exaggerated vigour which easily deceives overseas

---

[1] Jacob L. Mosak, in *Economic Reconstruction*, ed. Seymour E. Harris, pp. 90-1.
[2] A valuable contribution to this analysis is made by A. G. Hart in "Model-Building and Fiscal Policy", *American Economic Review*, September 1945, with a reply by Jacob Mosak in the same journal, March 1946.

observers. Many people in the United States are entirely sympathetic with the new anti-unemployment techniques which are now so widely supported in this country, and even if it were quite certain that their views would not prevail, there is no justification for the belief that the controllers of United States policy are sternly resolved to allow the trade cycle to run its course in future, as it appears often to have done in the past, without any serious effort to iron out its fluctuations. "It would be a mistake to assume that the desire for high employment is a discovery or a monopoly of any particular country, and that this desire is not shared in the United States",[1] and it would be a counsel of despair to ask us to base our own policy upon the hypothesis that the United States economy will inevitably return to the condition of chronic under-employment from which it suffered before the war. The experiences of the last twenty years have left a profound mark on United States thought, and though there is not the same consensus of opinion as in Great Britain as to the value of a co-ordinated policy for dealing with unemployment— and it should be noted that even in Great Britain the co-ordination may turn out in practice to be much less complete than some popular programmes would suggest—there can be little doubt that a good many unco-ordinated, but nevertheless partially effective, steps will be taken in the United States, first to prevent large-scale unemployment, and then to mitigate the effects of any decline in employment which may threaten. "In a sense, those who urge policies conducive to a high level of international trade on a multilateral basis must take it on faith that serious unemployment will not occur in the major industrial countries, and in particular in the United States, or that, if it does occur, the supply of dollars to the rest of the world will none the less be maintained."[2] Nor does the accep-

---

[1] L. Rasminsky, "Anglo-American Trade Prospects", *Economic Journal*, June-September 1945, p. 175.

[2] L. Rasminsky, loc. cit. It would be easy to find quotations from many American academic writers which would be relevant in this context, but sceptics are apt to put them aside as merely the personal and irresponsible opinions of men who have little or no real influence. The views of a Special Committee of the United States House of Representatives are, however, not to be so lightly dismissed. "The volume of world trade as a whole" the

tance of this view commit us to an attitude of irrational optimism in the field of employment policy such as we would feel embarrassed in adopting or commending in dealing with other fundamental problems. It is the normal experience in human affairs that the risks inherent in an attitude of this kind just have to be faced, and our everyday practice in dealing with other problems suggests that we should not be disappointed if we cannot get commitments quite as precise as we should like.

THE EMPLOYMENT ACT OF FEBRUARY, 1946

Doctrinaires who believe that there is only one path along which salvation is to be sought from the evils of economic instability will probably not be entirely reassured by the terms of the Employment Act which was approved by the Congress of the United States after a long struggle on February 20, 1946, and will no doubt be eager to contrast the vagueness of its language with the greater precision of the Murray-Wagner Bill which initiated the legislative debate on this subject, and of which the Act now accepted may seem to many a pale and ineffective reflection. Nevertheless, the significance of the mere existence of Congressional legislation on this subject should not be underestimated. It is surely a notable fact that it is now declared to be "the continuing policy and responsibility of the Federal Government to use all practicable means consistent with its needs and obligations and other essential considerations of national policy, with the assistance and co-operation of industry, agriculture, labour, and State and local governments, to co-ordinate and utilize all its plans, functions, and resources, for the purpose of creating and maintaining, in a manner

Committee stated, "is affected substantially by fluctuations in the United States demand for imports. By maintaining our demand at a high level, we can make a valuable contribution to world prosperity. An expansion of our imports constitutes, in fact, the greatest single contribution which we can make to world prosperity. Since our imports will be large only if we have a high level of domestic output and employment, our responsibility for world prosperity consists primarily in domestic policies which will insure a high and expanding output at home" (Sixth Report of the House Special Committee on Post-War Economic Policy and Planning. The Post-War Foreign Economic Policy of the United States. 79th Congress, 1st Session. House Report No. 541, 1945, p. 10).

calculated to foster and promote free competitive enterprise and the general welfare, conditions under which there will be afforded useful employment opportunities, including self-employment, for those able, willing, and seeking to work, and to promote maximum employment, production, and purchasing power." This language bears obvious marks of the struggle between those who wanted to go much further, and those who were reluctant to place upon the Federal Government any significant responsibility for the maintenance of satisfactory employment conditions. But even the most cynical critic is not entitled to maintain that this declaration has no meaning at all, and that the Government of the United States will, in future, be entirely passive in the face of any threat of widespread unemployment. There is now to be transmitted to each session of Congress an Economic Report upon levels of employment, production and purchasing power in the United States, which will review the economic programme of the Federal Government, and provide a programme for carrying out the policy which has been described above. A Council of Economic Advisers is to be constituted with the function of preparing the Economic Report, and a Joint Committee of both Houses is given the responsibility of making a continuing study of matters relating to the Report, and of submitting reports and recommendations thereon, to the Senate and the House of Representatives. There has been some disappointment that the Act does not prescribe beforehand the nature of the action to be taken in the future, but its terms are inconsistent with any hypothesis of continued and obstinate inaction.

It is certainly desirable that all Americans should appreciate more fully than some of them at present do, the peculiar importance which many in other countries attach to the maintenance of employment in the United States, and in particular to the relevance of this question to the smooth functioning of any multilateral trading system. There can have been few periods in history when the prosperity of any single country was such an obvious and direct interest of the whole of the rest of the world, as the prosperity of the United States is to-day. To any citizen of the United States, anxious that his country should make the most useful contribution possible to the welfare of other countries, it might be a slight exaggeration to say, "Make your own country as prosperous as possible", but the exaggeration would not be seriously misleading.

A lively interest in the maintenance of American prosperity which admits the diversity of the paths along which this end is likely to be sought and in some measure attained, is, however, a very different thing from the morbid interest sometimes displayed, which implicitly assumes, sometimes almost with a sense of satisfaction, that the American case is hopeless, and that nothing can be done about it. We cannot be sure that the United States will provide the conditions which the rest of the world would find most attractive, but equally there is no warrant for taking it for granted that nothing at all resembling these conditions will be forthcoming. Such pessimism, moreover, carries with it the further danger that, by a precipitate assumption that things will certainly go wrong, we may convert something which was merely a possibility into an unpleasant reality, towards the avoidance of which we might ourselves have made a useful contribution.

Those who are most sceptical of the capacity of the United States economy to maintain a reasonable degree of stability, naturally make a good deal of the divergent points of view from which many people in the United States and in Great Britain appear at the present time to interpret the significance of post-war export trade. The purpose which many Americans tend to have in mind when they dilate upon the value of large-scale exports, financed perhaps by the machinery of international investment, is the maintenance during the difficult post-war transition period of an adequate level of employment. Such ideas are not entirely foreign to British ways of thinking, but in our present abnormal situation we are naturally much more conscious of the function of exports as the means for paying for imports whose absence would impose the most serious inconvenience upon us. It is not difficult to demonstrate the inadequacy of international loans, by themselves, to solve the United States employment problem, but we should not on that account hastily write down the importance of United States foreign lending or exaggerate the difficulties which in the course of time may arise from the failure to adjust other sectors of American international economic policy to the logical, and in the long run unavoidable, requirements of the status of an international creditor. The world is in desperate need of capital rehabilitation, and without extensive United States loans this need can be satisfied only very inadequately. The sooner the United States economy is adjusted to the admission of an import surplus, the better it will be for everybody, including the people of the United States themselves. It is, however, perhaps too much to expect revolutionary reversals of policy, and large-scale foreign lending which was not liable to sudden interruptions would permit reforms which, in their early stages, would be more modest to be carried through in more orderly fashion, and with a reasonable hope that, in the course of time, they would be pushed still further and ultimately produce a balanced situation adequate for the purpose. We should welcome any means which would cushion the shock of a radical re-orientation of United States policy, especially if in so doing we could also avoid an intolerable slowing down in the tempo of economic development in other directions.

THE BRETTON WOODS AGREEMENTS

Turning now to a consideration of the significance of the various international institutions whose erection has recently been widely discussed, and in some cases already formally proposed, we are dealing with possibilities which, in many respects, are more concrete and definite. By the end of 1945, the constitutional processes for ratifying the two Agreements embodied in the Annexes to the Final Act of the Bretton Woods Conference of July 1944 had been completed in the United States, the United Kingdom and a sufficient number of other countries, to assure the 65 per cent of the total assigned quotas which had been prescribed as a condition precedent to the formal establishment of the International Monetary Fund and the International Bank of Reconstruction and Development. The Boards of Directors of these two institutions have already held their first meetings, so that they have now definitely passed beyond the stages of speculation and discussion, and are ready to become normal working parts of a new international economic system.

This is not the appropriate place for an exhaustive analysis of all the implications of the Bretton Woods Agreements.[1] Several of the international safeguards which we have been discussing are, however, either in part or in whole, guaranteed by the acceptance of these Agreements. "Alterations of the exchange rate have been, so to speak, legalized as being in certain situations quite legitimate, so that they have lost their character of a declaration of bankruptcy",[2] and at the same time, the principle that national decisions on this point are matters of exclusively domestic concern has also been accepted, so that the machinery of the Fund affords valuable protection against employment instability due to the unco-ordinated depreciation of national currencies. Especially in the United States, some critics have complained that the latitude permitted to members of the Fund was still too great, and would even have preferred to ban exchange rate fluctuations altogether. The acceptance of such a rigid rule as this, has, however, never been at all seriously considered. Experience of the frustrating effects of exchange depreciation during the Great Depression has cured many people of the belief that this was a specific upon which they could always confidently fall back in times of trouble; very few, however, would approve of their governments binding themselves in no circumstances to alter the external value of their currency. Much of the current discussion of the adequacy of this section of the Bretton Woods programme is naturally concerned with the limitations imposed upon the freedom of our own economy to choose, at its own discretion, the path which it is to follow. But, as we have already seen, from the standpoint of the unemployment risks generated outside our own economy, it is of at least equal

---

[1] For a more elaborate analysis, which leads to conclusions similar to those defended in the present study, the reader should refer to R. F. Harrod's *A Page of British Folly*, London, Macmillan, 1946.

[2] Dag Hammarskjöld, "From Bretton Woods to Full Employment", *Index*, December 1945, p. 15.

importance to offset against any apparent inconvenience which such limitations upon our freedom might imply the substantial benefits arising from an assurance that other economies, subject to a similar discipline, would to a significant extent be debarred from embarrassing us by similar free decisions on their side.

From the point of view of our present study, the most significant general problem raised by the Bretton Woods proposals is, however, the provision of adequate international reserves, access to which would protect member states following full employment policies from such shortages of overseas assets as might compel them to restrict their international contacts, and adopt foreign exchange controls inconsistent with the maintenance of a multilateral international trading system. Among the purposes of the International Monetary Fund is "to assist in the establishment of a multilateral system of payments in respect of current transactions between members and in the elimination of foreign exchange restrictions which hamper the growth of world trade". It was recognized that, for many economies, this objective cannot be realized at once. Accordingly, "in the post-war transitional period, members may maintain and adapt to changing circumstances restrictions on payments and transfers for current international transactions". It is seldom easy to predict the probable exact length of such a "transitional period". If it were to be indefinitely prolonged, the Fund would clearly be a failure. It was implied in the original constitution of the International Monetary Fund, that five years from the date at which the Fund began its operations might be accepted as a rough guess as the probable length of this period. Any member which, after that date, still retained restrictions which were inconsistent with the general obligations of membership, was required to consult the Fund as to their further retention, and the Fund was entitled to make representations that conditions were favourable for their withdrawal. Any member which then persisted in maintaining restrictions inconsistent with the purposes of the Fund, might be declared ineligible to use its resources.[1] For Great

---

[1] Articles XIV, 4; XV, 2a.

Britain, however, the Financial Agreement of 1945 has substantially shortened this transitional period of freedom. Not later than one year after the effective date of the Agreement, the United Kingdom has now agreed to make the sterling receipts from current transactions of all sterling area countries freely available for current transactions in any currency area without discrimination, though the Agreement also provides that, in exceptional cases, a later date may be agreed upon after consultation.

In relation to this broad problem, two general lines of criticism have been directed against the Bretton Woods proposals. It has been argued, in the first place, that they imply an exaggeration of the importance of mere financial machinery, and that it was unreasonable to expect the United Kingdom to undertake long-term policy commitments, however qualified and indefinite in the date of their effective operation, until assurances had also been given about other no less important issues. In particular, it was said, we should know more about the commercial policies of other countries, and still more urgent, much more about the methods likely to be available to us for relaxing the peculiar, but extremely pressing and difficult, short-term pressures which are the natural preoccupation of statesmen in many countries whose economies have been violently disrupted by the requirements of the war. And it has been objected, in the second place, that in any event, the resources to be made available to either the Fund or the Bank will be inadequate for the purposes in mind.

There was a good deal of force in the first contention, so far at least as it applied to the absence of definite arrangements for handling the transitional difficulties of economies with abnormal accumulations of war indebtedness. It is not intended that the Monetary Fund should provide facilities for post-war relief or deal with international indebtedness arising out of the war, and while the Bank for Reconstruction and Development is expected to help in the restoration of economies destroyed or disrupted by the war, and the reconversion of productive facilities to peace-time needs, it too is debarred from taking responsibility for obligations arising from the war. An awkward gap therefore remained in any picture which might have been formed at the time of the Bretton Woods Conference, of the institutional structure sketched up to that date for facilitating postwar economic reconstruction on a more or less permanent basis.

It was, however, always a little unfair to the sponsors of the Bretton Woods proposals to suggest that they were indifferent to the inevitably incomplete character of the solution which they were offering. A resolution of the Conference itself formally recognized that "the complete attainment of the purposes and objectives stated in the Agreement cannot be achieved through the instrumentality of the Fund alone", and urged upon Governments the duty of reaching "agreement as soon as possible on ways and means whereby they may best (1) reduce obstacles to international trade and in other ways promote mutually advantageous international commercial relations; (2) bring about the orderly marketing of staple commodities at prices fair to the producer and consumer alike; (3) deal with the special problems of international concern which will arise from the cessation of production for war purposes; and (4) facilitate by co-operative effort the harmonization of national policies of Member States, designed to promote and maintain high levels of employment and progressively rising standards of living." There is, no doubt, always a risk that those who have long devoted the whole of their time and thoughts to the preparation of an elaborate piece of international machinery may come imperceptibly to cherish for its own sake the instrument which they tend to regard as peculiarly their own creation, and thus to discount unduly the importance of parallel and simultaneous action in other fields, of the urgent necessity for which they may, merely as a matter of logic, be quite well aware. No one, however, ever seriously supposed that instruments of the kind outlined at Bretton Woods could by themselves provide more than a subordinate part of what was needed to get a world economy working on reasonably stable lines. But in dealing with such a complicated problem, it was necessary to start somewhere. The future historian of the war period may know more than we at present do of the reasons which induced the leading governments concerned to carry forward discussions in the fields of exchange policy and the organization of international invest-ment, while other no less important discussions were lagging behind. There is certainly nothing in the Bretton Woods proposals themselves which was calculated to encourage these delays, and if things had gone the other way, and instead of the Bretton Woods Final Act we had been asked first to discuss the ratification of an agreement dealing with some other equally important problem, those who in any event are luke-warm about such matters would no doubt have been found urging caution on the ground that nothing definite had yet been settled about exchange rates or the prospects for inter-national lending.

In any event, the proposals associated with the announcement of the Financial Agreement in December 1945 go at least some distance in the direction of filling in the gaps to which the critics had pointed. There have naturally been sharp differences of opinion as to the adequacy of the proposals for either purpose; in particular, some time must elapse before the content of the proposed agreement on commercial policy and other related matters reaches a stage of definiteness com-parable with that registered at Bretton Woods, and in the meantime formal commitments have to be made on monetary and exchange policy. There has also been much criticism of the measures proposed for dealing with the transitional period. But at least some action of great importance is now definitely contemplated, and no one can now complain that the complex interrelationships of all these issues have received no more than formal recognition.

The objection that the Bretton Woods instruments will be equipped with funds inadequate for the purposes in mind is of a more concrete kind. It must be admitted that the figure actually arrived at can scarcely have been the result of anything more than the roughest of guesses. On the assumption that countries not represented at Bretton Woods would later be admitted to membership, the aggregate subscriptions to both the Fund and the Bank would amount in either case to the equivalent of 10 billion dollars, a figure which has to be justified more on account of its convenient roundness than by any careful analysis of probable requirements. A considerable fraction of the total will, moreover, be subscribed in currencies for which there is in any case unlikely to be much demand from Great Britain, while the aggregate, of course, necessarily greatly exceeds the amount available at any one time to meet the needs of any single economy. If the ideas embodied in the so-called Keynes plan had been favourably received in the United States, the liquid resources of the Monetary Fund would no doubt have been greater, and the conditions limiting the full use at one time of the whole of its resources would also have been less stringent. But though there is no peculiar sanctity about the figure now embodied in the Bretton Woods Final Act, it was scarcely possible to arrive at an appropriate estimate by any other method. In forming a judgment about their own probable position as members of the International Monetary Fund, some countries have, naturally enough, attempted to compare the size of the quota allotted to them with the volume of reserves which, if it had been available at the time, might have saved them from embarrassment during the worst period of their history. It was scarcely to be expected, however, that the quotas of all, or indeed of any country, could have been determined on any such basis as this. If a situation were to recur in which many countries needed assistance on the same scale as during the most difficult days of the Great Depression, that fact alone would indicate that the Monetary Fund had failed. Its purpose is to prevent the recurrence of such situations by making assistance available at a suitably early date. And in taking such action the Fund must, of course, be assisted by suitable action in the other fields with which the Bretton Woods Conference was not directly concerned.

Especially in relation to the operations of the Bank, it is, moreover, important to bear in mind that the volume of resources likely to be made available to suitable borrowers as a result of the Bank's activities is not necessarily limited to the funds actually placed at its disposal. Its work may reasonably be expected to create conditions sufficiently favourable to encourage a flow of international investment for which it need not itself take any direct responsibility, so that any estimate of the Bank's fertilizing potentialities, both direct and indirect, which was based upon consideration of its own resources only, would be misleading.

The possibility of an embarrassing shortage of international reserves, and in particular of United States dollars, of course remains, and the Bretton Woods Final Act included provisions designed to meet this eventuality. Article VII of the Agreement of the International Monetary Fund provides that if a general scarcity of a particular currency is developing, the Fund may propose to the member concerned that additional supplies of its currency should be lent to the Fund, or require it to sell its currency to the Fund for any gold which the Fund may have accumulated. If these measures prove inadequate, the Fund may in the last resort formally declare the currency in question "scarce", whereupon other members are authorized temporarily to impose limitations on the freedom of exchange operations in the scarce currency.

The United States dollar is obviously the currency which, in the view of most people, is most likely to become "scarce", and Article VII may therefore be interpreted as an assurance to other countries that, if United States policy creates embarrassment for them in their international economic relations, restrictive action on their part, which is highly repugnant to the United States, and which it is one of the general objectives of the Fund to eliminate, would nevertheless in these circumstances be regarded as in accordance with the requirements of good international behaviour. The effectiveness of the Article will, of course, largely depend on the extent to which it is found unnecessary to put into operation at least its more stringent sections. A country whose currency had formally been declared to be "scarce" would thereby be clearly marked out as failing adequately to discharge its responsibilities as a member of an orderly international economic system, and there can be little doubt that it was the intention of those responsible for proposing the procedure embodied in this Article, that the odium which such a formal identification would carry with it would be sufficient to ensure that no important economy would ever allow itself to be placed in such a position, and that if ever it threatened to occur, adequate steps would be taken to relieve the shortage.

The constitution of the International Monetary Fund gives formal recognition to the right to safeguard balances of payments against disruptive international movements of capital, by providing that "members may exercise such controls as are necessary to regulate international capital movements",[1] provided that such controls do not restrict payments for current transactions or unduly delay transfers of funds in settlement of commitments. Indeed, in certain circumstances, the Fund may itself request a member to impose such controls where "a large or sustained outflow of capital" threatens to divert the normal flow of the Fund's resources, whose use for meeting such an outflow is prohibited, and a member who, after being so requested, fails to exercise appropriate controls may be declared ineligible to use the resources of the Fund.[2] Exchange control, as applied to capital movements, thus becomes approved and respectable conduct in the code of international good behaviour.

The operations of the proposed International Bank for Reconstruction and Development are directly relevant to the determination of the general level of world demand, but might at first sight appear to have less significance for the maintenance of a stable level of demand for British exports, which is the international requirement of most direct concern for British full employment policy. It would, however, be quite consistent with the terms of the Articles under which the Bank will be required to carry on its work, for its resources to be so used as greatly to assist the maintenance of stability in the economies from which the greater part of the funds available for international investment are likely to be drawn, and though the Bank has no instructions to work with this objective formally in view, the suggestion is of sufficient importance to merit separate consideration here.[3]

[1] Article VI, Section 3.
[2] Article VI, Section 1.
[3] A fuller and more elaborate discussion of this point may be found in Eugene Staley's *World Economic Development*, International Labour Office, 1944.

Fluctuations in employment are normally associated in the closest possible way with fluctuations in the demand for capital equipment, and it is a commonplace to suggest measures for stabilizing this demand as a central feature in programmes for the prevention of unemployment. The large-scale projects of development in "backward" areas, for which it is hoped that directly or indirectly the International Bank will be responsible, will necessarily require a lengthy period of time before they can be in full operation. It is therefore natural to inquire whether the needs of these areas might not still be adequately met, if in determining the timing of these development projects, account were also to be taken of the desirability of offsetting any threatened contraction in the internal demand for capital equipment which seemed likely to occur in the more advanced countries, from whom the capital equipment of the "backward" areas would mainly be drawn. "Inducements would be offered to schedule the orders for equipment to be used in development programmes so as to canalize this demand towards those particular industries and those particular localities which at any given time might be depressed, and so as to step up the total volume of equipment orders in periods of actual or threatened general depression."[1] The normal practice of the past has been rather to stimulate the purchase of capital equipment from the advanced countries for use in undeveloped areas during boom years, so that investment in their development has often helped to unstabilize rather than to stabilize the economies of the world. The suggestion now is that this practice should be reversed, and that developmental purchases of equipment should instead be consciously organized in a counter-cyclical manner.

The same principle could equally well be applied to cushion the effects of the violent fluctuations in demand necessarily associated with the transition from war to peace conditions, and thus help in maintaining stability of employment during the immediate post-war era.

There is perhaps some danger in speculations of this kind of falling into the error of regarding the inhabitants of "backward"

[1] Staley, op. cit., pp. 92-3.

areas as merely passive instruments conveniently provided to be used for the benefit of the more advanced economies, who, having registered no more than an indifferent success in solving problems for which they must themselves be regarded as being primarily responsible, would thus be enabled to look elsewhere for convenient ways of escape from their troubles. But while it is proper to remind ourselves of this danger, there is in principle no good reason why the process of international investment should not be beneficial to all the parties concerned in this no less than in other respects.

It is also worthy of notice that the constitution of the International Bank for Reconstruction and Development specifically provides that "the Bank shall impose no conditions that the proceeds of a loan shall be spent in the territories of any particular member or members."[1] The formal renunciation by this provision of "tied loans" constitutes a safeguard of great importance against the risk that the flow of a large part of the dollar supplies made available to the rest of the world shall be so canalized as seriously to impede the development of sound well-balanced multilateral trading relations.

THE INTERNATIONAL CONFERENCE ON TRADE AND EMPLOYMENT

In relation to international collaboration in fields other than monetary and investment policy, official action has for a variety of reasons been more cautious, and international institutions for the harmonization of national commercial policies cannot yet be discussed with a formal text before us with the same status such as Bretton Woods provided for the purposes we have already discussed. The intentions which had from time to time been announced to initiate parallel action in other fields have, however, been carried a definite stage further by the proposal for the creation of an International Trade Organization of the United Nations, which forms an important part of the Proposals for Consideration by an International Conference on Trade and Employment of December 6, 1945, and whose general purpose is described as the promotion of "national and international action for the expansion of the production, exchange

[1] Article III, Section 5 (a).

and consumption of goods, for the reduction of tariffs and other trade barriers, and for the elimination of all forms of discriminatory treatment in international commerce, thus contributing to an expanding world economy, to the establishment and maintenance in all countries of high levels of employment and real income, and to the creation of economic conditions conducive to the maintenance of world peace". Since, as the Proposals put it, the expansion of trade which is essential for maximum levels of employment, production and consumption "can only be attained by collective measures, in continuous operation and adaptable to economic changes, it is necessary to establish permanent machinery for international collaboration in matters affecting international commerce, with a view to continuous consultation, the provision of expert advice, the formulation of agreed policies, procedures and plans, and to the development of agreed rules of conduct in regard to matters affecting international trade", and it is proposed that the members of the International Trade Organization should "undertake to conduct their international commercial policies and relations in accordance with agreed principles to be set forth in the articles of the Organization". We shall of course, be obliged to give the most careful scrutiny to the details of any agreement which may emerge from the conference charged with the responsibility of drawing up the constitution of this Organization. The Proposals of December 1945 set forth an elaborate outline which will presumably form a basis for the agenda of the conference. The Proposals, it is stated, "have the endorsement of the Executive branch of the Government of the United States", while "equally, the Government of the United Kingdom is in full agreement on all important points in these proposals and accepts them as a basis for international discussion". While, nevertheless, there can be no certainty that the principles which will ultimately emerge will correspond in every particular with the published outline, the intention is clearly to cover a wide range of territory, including not only commercial policy in the ordinary sense, but also the principles to be observed by members engaged in State trading in any form, provision for "the curbing of restrictive trade practices resulting from private international business arrangements", and principles to "govern the institution and operation of inter-governmental commodity arrangements". The ground covered by any rules of international conduct which might emerge from the deliberations of the proposed Conference would indeed be a good deal wider than anything suggested by our special concern for the level of employment in Great Britain, but the potential effects of each one of them in that field might be quite substantial. It cannot be taken as a matter of course that the constitution of the new organization will adequately meet all the requirements of British policy, but at least all the important issues have now been raised in such a way as to justify the expectation that some substantial progress will be registered.

The proposed outline of principles is least precise in dealing with the old-fashioned but still highly important problem of tariffs. In this field, indeed, little more is said than has already been registered in Article VII of the Mutual Aid Agreement. In the light of the principles set forth in this Article, it is said, "members should enter into arrangements for the substantial reduction of tariffs and for the elimination of tariff preferences, action for the elimination of tariff preferences being taken in conjunction with adequate measures for the substantial reduction of barriers to world trade." The definition of "adequate" in this context will be no easy matter, but it is perhaps in dealing with tariffs that one can see most clearly the practical limitations imposed by the effort to discover general principles capable of universal application everywhere. We should not indeed be greatly astonished if at the International Conference which is to be summoned, more than one country were to be found passionately defending its own trade barriers as having a peculiarly justifiable character arising from the unique circumstances of the economy. Many such claims should be heavily discounted; it is nevertheless true that arithmetically uniform reductions of tariff rates would entirely fail to produce equality of treatment. There is not necessarily any high degree of correlation between the international restrictiveness of a tariff rate and its arithmetical level. Provided therefore that the final result is "adequate", there is a strong case here for the widest possible range of flexibility, even if the list of formally agreed principles may appear disappointingly meagre.

The efficient working of a multilateral international economic system demands that sooner or later the United States should adjust its commercial policy to the requirements of an international creditor status, in other words, permit an import surplus to emerge as a normal feature of its economy. The principles of the new organization will naturally and properly be set forth in general terms applicable to the economies of all its members; nevertheless most people outside the United States, as well as many inside, will equally naturally inquire first how far they are likely to contribute to the achievement of this specific objective. There has sometimes been some justification for the view that too many people in the United States, even among those who were not insensitive to the needs of the new international situation which has been rapidly developing, were unduly complacent in believing that action of the kind authorized by the Reciprocal Trade Agreements Act, first passed in 1934 and subsequently several times renewed, was sufficient for the discharge of United States responsibility in building up a stable international trading system. Even if the most favourable view is taken of the effects of the Agreements made in terms of this Act, it still remains true that their importance has been very limited, and indeed that the restrictions imposed upon United States negotiators by the terms of the Act effectively preclude them from dealing with the situation in a genuinely radical way. In certain important directions, indeed, the possibilities of action under existing legislation had already been exhausted when the Act came up for renewal in 1945, and whatever success the Agreements may have had in relaxing some of the trade restrictions imposed during the Depression, their effect upon the balance between United States exports and United States imports had been practically negligible.

There had, however, already before the end of 1945, been some encouraging indications that the importance of these limitations was being more clearly and widely recognized, and the approval given to the amended form in which the Trade Agreements Act was renewed in 1945 shows that at least it was no longer generally assumed that the facilities of the original Act were sufficient. United States negotiators are now authorized to offer a reduction of duties to a level of 50 per cent lower than that current at the time the Act was renewed, so that for commodities upon which duties have already been reduced in terms of the Act of 1934, it is now possible to contemplate a reduction of as much as 75 per cent, as compared with the usually high level prevailing at that time.

Observers in Great Britain may also be usefully reminded that the significance of amendments of the United States tariff is not to be measured solely in terms of the wider outlets which might thus be afforded for British exports in the United States market. The much more important point is the provision of wider outlets in the United States for imports in general. The commercial relations of Great Britain and the United States have traditionally been based upon a multilateral foundation, a large part of the dollar supply needed to finance British purchases in the United States arising as a result of United States imports from third countries. The changes in the structure of post-war world trade are unlikely to be so far-reaching as to make these triangular or multilateral exchanges less convenient in the future to all the parties concerned.

How far can the Proposals of December 1945 be interpreted as a firm commitment on the part of the United States Government to press for still more decisive movement in the direction indicated by the amended Trade Agreements Act? "In accepting these principles" it has been said, "the United States on its part would pledge itself to seek further lowering of its tariffs through bargaining under the Reciprocal Trade Agreements Act".[1] What this rather narrow interpretation might mean in practice, has still to be tested. Even amended and liberalized as it has been, the scope of effective action permitted by the Trade Agreements Act would, however, almost certainly be too narrow to cover everything that is needed in this field. Nevertheless, it is significant that in amending the Act the

[1] *Bulletin of National City Bank of New York,* January 1946, p. 7.

United States should have already, on its own initiative, taken a fairly decisive step of a kind which a few years ago would have seemed almost impossible.

The Proposals include also an outline of the institutional machinery to be placed at the disposal of the International Trade Organization. Provided that the constitution is kept free from unnecessarily hampering restrictions, it usually happens in such cases that the effectiveness of the machinery will depend in practice very much upon the initiative and tactful skill of those who are first placed in charge of it, and while we must again await the final result before we can be certain that the new institution will be permitted to undertake useful and fundamental work, the outline, as it stands at present, does not appear to be unduly restrictive.

A UNITED NATIONS TRADE COMMISSION

We may, however, illustrate some of the activities in which the secretariat of such an institution might usefully engage by referring to some of the ideas which have recently been current in the United States on this subject. It should be remembered that the provision of safeguards against instability of employment is not the sole or even the primary purpose of an international trade organization. It aims in the first instance at facilitating a general expansion of trade which would be quite compatible with considerable fluctuations in its volume. Nevertheless, the administration of a code of international rules for the general regulation of commercial policy could properly, and without great difficulty, also take into account the desirability of reducing the fluctuations in general demand which are the immediate causes of unemployment, and in particular, could afford protection against the risks of unforeseeable or sudden changes in national policy.

Professor Bidwell has proposed[1] that a United Nations Trade Commission should be served by experts engaged continuously in studying the possibilities of the most effective utilization of the world's resources through a steadily expanding volume of

---

[1] "The Expansion of International Trade" in *The United States in a Multilateral Economy*, New York, Council on Foreign Relations, 1945, Chap. VII.

international trade. At the same time, there should be continuous examination of the economic and political effects of commercial policies, tariffs, customs administration and all legislative or administrative measures which restrict or regulate imports and exports. On the administrative side, the Commission should be concerned with the task of making effective the provisions of the multilateral convention, providing a means for hearing complaints and adjusting minor disputes, and perhaps granting temporary exemptions from the obligations of the convention in accordance with stated criteria, and suggesting amendments which experience had shown to be desirable.

Much of the work of an organization of this kind could not be fully effective until after the lapse of a considerable period of time, and it is perhaps partly on this account that suggestions in this field have tended to excite a less lively interest than other proposals from which prompter results might be expected. Many of the most troublesome obstructions from which the urgent problems which seem to demand instant handling arise are, however, often the result of prolonged neglect of some important basic change in the background of production and consumption, and the contribution which might be made to the smooth working of any international economic system by an organization to whom was entrusted the specific task of maintaining a continuous survey of this background could be of the greatest importance.

INTERNATIONAL EMPLOYMENT POLICY

The business of the proposed International Conference on Trade and Employment has been outlined in greatest detail in relation to the constitution and activities of the International Trade Organization. But though the Proposals Concerning Employment are much briefer, they also indicate the possibility of formal safeguards in this field too. It is proposed that the nations represented at the Conference should subscribe to an undertaking by which each of them would agree to "take action designed to achieve and maintain full employment within its own jurisdiction, through measures appropriate to its political and economic institutions", to refrain from seeking "to maintain employment through measures which are likely to create unemployment in other countries, or which are incompatible with international undertakings designed to promote an expanding volume of international trade and investment in accordance with comparative efficiencies of production", to "make arrangements, both individually and collaboratively, for the collection, analysis, and exchange of information on employment problems, trends, and policies", and to "consult regularly on employment problems and hold special conferences in case of threat of widespread unemployment". There is a great deal of detail to be filled in before the real significance of these undertakings can be precisely determined. Even if they are not watered down at the Conference, they probably do not, as they stand at present, go so far as the Australian proposals to the International Labour Conference. Nevertheless, some general resolutions which governments may be expected to ratify will no doubt emerge from the Conference, and a formal convention imposing obligations which would satisfy even those who are most fearful of the effects of membership of an open international economic system is not to be ruled out as quite impossible. On the whole, however, it seems more probable that the form of any international agreement likely to be reached in the near future will be such that for really effective assurances of the kind which we have been discussing, Great Britain will have to rely upon a number of rather loosely related measures, of varied content, involving varied degrees of formal obligations, and almost certainly leaving some awkward unfilled gaps.

THE ANGLO-AMERICAN LOAN AGREEMENT

The credit of $4,400 millions, including $650 millions as a final settlement of all outstanding lend-lease obligations, which is the kernel of the Financial Agreement of December 1945, is an instrument of major importance in providing Great Britain with the assurances needed to justify the belief that the attempt to establish a new open international economic system will not founder on the rocks of the immediate post-war transitional strains. The Agreement, which has also served as a model for the similar Canadian credit of $1,250 millions announced in March 1946, has been accepted by the British Government and

Parliament, and now awaits ratification by the United States Congress. A full discussion of all the issues raised by this Proposal falls outside the scope of the present study. Some of the same difficulties present themselves here as have already been discussed in relation to the Bretton Woods quotas. With so many imponderable but highly relevant uncertainties, we can in such matters at best expect little more than a rough guess. We are, however, entitled to claim that, whether imperfectly or not, substantial provision has now been offered to meet all the major peculiar external difficulties of the British economy as it seeks in the post-war world to maintain a high level of employment.

The proposal examined earlier in our study for guarantees from the more important economies of stability in their aggregate demand for imports finds a modest place in the Proposals of December 1945, in the suggestion that "members having a complete State monopoly of foreign trade should undertake to purchase annually from members, on a non-discriminatory basis, products valued at not less than an aggregate amount to be agreed upon", though there is at present no hint that this idea might, with advantage, be carried any further. The "escape" clauses of the Financial Agreement may, however, also be interpreted as a partial application of the same general principle. In the event of an unfavourable balance of payments situation arising, Great Britain is to be relieved from part of the financial obligations arising from acceptance of the loan, a provision, however, which offers protection only in the event of the international demand for imports actually proving inadequate, and involves no positive obligation to maintain the general level of demand. These "escape" clauses were, indeed, designed primarily as a measure of insurance against the embarrassments which easily arise in discharging, over a long period, the financial obligations implied in the acceptance of a large international loan, embarrassments which experience has often shown may be very great, even for those who are not greatly concerned with the risks of unemployment. Their relevance to the maintenance of full employment is also obvious enough.

The first official indication that safeguards of this kind were receiving serious consideration came from Canada. The Canadian Government, in view of the peculiar structure of the Canadian economy, has naturally been concerned lest the post-war balance of payments problems of Great Britain and her European allies "should lead to the establishment, even on a temporary basis, of currency or trade blocs applying discriminatory treatment to their trade with other countries", and the Canadian Minister of Reconstruction declared in April 1945 that his Government was therefore "willing to extend to such countries, to enable them to accomplish this transition, adequate credits to finance, to the degree necessary, their import requirements from Canada. In the view of the Government, appropriate terms for the repayment of these credits would recognize unequivocally the dependence of such international debt payments on the expansion of world trade and ample markets for the exports by which credits must be repaid."[1]

The proposals of December 1945 formally recognized this principle in the elaborate provisions of Article V of the Financial Agreement between the Governments of the United States and the United Kingdom. It is therein provided that "in any year in which the Government of the United Kingdom requests the Government of the United States to waive the amount of the interest due" upon the credit whose provision is the main purpose of the agreement, "in view of the present and prospective conditions of international exchange and the level of its gold and foreign exchange reserves", the Government of the United States will grant the waiver if "the income of the United Kingdom from home-produced exports, plus its net income from invisible current transactions in its balance of payments, was on the average over the five preceding calendar years less than the average annual amount of United Kingdom imports during 1936-8, fixed at £866 million, as such figure may be adjusted for changes in the price level of these imports." In broad outline, the intention is that an economy which has accepted international credits to help it through the post-war

---

[1] *Employment and Income with special reference to the Initial Period of Reconstruction*, pp. 8-9.

transitional period should be afforded some protection, not against the occurrence of fluctuations of international demand for their exports, but against the risk that such fluctuations may seriously derange their balance of payments if the acceptance of international credits were presumed to carry with it a firm obligation in all circumstances to meet the interest charges involved.

The same principle is given expression in similar terms in Article 4 of the Canadian Loan Agreement, announced on March 7, 1946, whereby the Government of Canada has agreed to provide the Government of the United Kingdom with a credit of $1,250,000,000 on conditions which, in all essential respects, are identical with those of the American loan announced in December 1945.

There are some unpleasant similarities between such an arrangement and the imposition of a "means test" in relation to internal economic policy, and we know what psychological and social tensions the imposition of such a test often arouses. If an "escape clause" of this kind were to become a part of the normal international machinery for the transitional period, there would be obvious advantages in making its application as automatic and as little subject to discretion as possible. An attempt has been made in the Financial Agreement with the United States to realize this condition by providing that the International Monetary Fund should assume responsibility for certifying to the movement of the United Kingdom balance of payments, as indicated in Article 5 of the Agreement which has been quoted above. For it would be one of the incidental benefits of the establishment of the Fund to create an adequate and objective statistical service which would quickly reveal changes in the balance of payments in terms which were not seriously open to question, a service, moreover, in whose administration each of the interested parties would presumably be playing an active and continuous part. In any event, any embarrassment we might feel about submitting our international financial position to the scrutiny of an external authority should be mitigated by the reflection that embarrassments no less serious, if somewhat different in character, would almost necessarily arise for our partners in any regional system which we might hope to operate as a substitute and under our own control.

The Proposals contain a further safeguard for those who are sensitive to the risks of adverse balances of payments. While members of the International Trade Organization are to be required "not to maintain any quotas, embargoes, or other quantitative restrictions on their export or import trade with other members", there is a supplementary provision that "members confronted with an adverse balance of payments should be entitled to impose quantitative import restrictions, as an aid to the restoration of equilibrium in the balance of payments . . . under conditions and procedures to be agreed upon." Obviously, a conclusion to the process of "agreement" may not be reached without considerable difficulty and much hard bargaining. Nevertheless, an important principle is here recognized which, whatever the precise form in which it is finally embodied, should go some way towards allaying the fears of those who are sceptical about the possibility of reconciling full employment policies with an open international economic system in the world as it is to-day.

Chapter X

THE ALTERNATIVES TO AN OPEN SYSTEM

HAVE WE ANY REAL FREEDOM OF CHOICE?

THE title of this Chapter may perhaps be criticized as implying a much wider range of alternatives open for our unfettered choice than is in fact available to us. In an important sense, the acceptance of the Financial Agreement of December 1945 might be interpreted as settling the issue with which we are here concerned in favour of an open international system, and some in Great Britain who have approved of this decision have felt that in the circumstances no other choice was effectively open to them.

This may not, however, finally dispose of the matter. An Englishman who believes that "we cannot survive without the methods that are called 'reciprocal' by those who practise them and 'bilateral' by those who object"[1] is, it would appear, obliged to draw the further conclusion that the "logic of events" will ultimately show the arrangements now proposed and formally accepted to be unworkable, and that eventually we shall be driven back, whether we like it or not, to some quite different method of organizing our international economic relations.

It is indeed always wise constantly to remind ourselves that, much as we might like to remould the pattern of international economic relations according to the principles which appear to us most rational, in real life intractable facts are always limiting the freedom of our choice, and that it may therefore be a merely academic exercise to list all the alternatives which are theoretically conceivable, as if we should then be able to choose any one from the list that happened to appeal most to us. On the other hand, it may be argued with much plausibility that in dealing with such complex problems there is seldom any clearly defined moment of decision, when we consciously and deliberately decide to move along one path or another. As a

[1] *The Economist*, December 15, 1945, p. 850.

rule, we make a series of limited *ad hoc* decisions, no one of which may appear at the time to commit us irrevocably to any general line of policy, and then looking back we may discover that the fundamental decision has already been taken, almost without our being aware of it. Whether or not the decisions of December 1945 represent a final and decisive stage in the evolution of our economic policy from which there can be no turning back is a question likely for some time to come to be disputed.

Upon the concrete implications of these considerations there will, in any particular situation, be a wide divergence of opinion, but our use here of the title, The Alternatives to an Open System, should not be interpreted as indicating any lack of appreciation of the fact that our freedom of choice at any point of time is always severely limited by many events which have already occurred and cannot be reversed.

Nevertheless, our deference to "realism" would be carried much too far if it led us to deny that we had any freedom of choice at all. A prudent statesman will always resolutely "face the facts", but he will not ask others to believe that he is merely the creature of circumstance, entirely lacking any capacity to influence the course of events. It is natural to be tempted to strengthen the case for the line of policy which we happen to favour by arguing that no alternative is possible, and those who feel themselves responsible for past decisions which are later called in question find comfort in the belief that in the circumstances they could not have done otherwise. But despite the real and far-reaching limitations upon our freedom of choice, such reasoning is seldom completely convincing. At the very worst, there is usually a narrow margin within which we have a real freedom to choose, and especially when the margin is a little wider than this, we do well to remind ourselves that if in future our freedom may appear to have diminished, it may be on account of *ad hoc* decisions on particular issues taken to-day.

The attempt to reconstruct a new open international system, with due regard to the new factors in the post-war world situation, may conceivably fail for a wide variety of reasons.

The contingency with which, however, we are most particularly concerned is that for the British economy the demands made by the new system may prove to be irreconcilable with the adjustments which, in any event, must be made as a result of the wartime changes in Great Britain's financial position and of the overriding obligation to assure full employment within our own economy. Such a failure would, of course, be quite consistent with the maintenance of a large volume of international trade, and in some respects it may be a little misleading to assume that the conditions under which trade would then be conducted were properly to be described in terms of a "system". There would certainly be a large number of *ad hoc* and constantly varying arrangements which would scarcely deserve such a title, though in this respect the contrast with a reconstituted open system can easily be overstated, for a new open order would also probably not conform at all closely to the requirements of strict logic.

REGIONAL TRADE REGULATION

The number of alternative possibilities is, in theory, very large. We need not attempt here, however, any exhaustive classification of all these hypothetical "systems". Much will depend on the general character of the national economies which emerge during the period of post-war reconstruction. We might, for example, attempt to outline the international picture which would present itself if a large number of countries were to model their economies upon the same principles as those of the U.S.S.R. But many of the theoretical possibilities have little practical significance, and while prophecy is now even a more risky enterprise than is usual in a highly uncertain world, it is fairly safe to assume that most of the variants worth discussing to-day will conform more or less closely to one or two easily recognizable patterns. Any such radical break with the past as we have just mentioned is not very likely, and we may confine our discussion here to arrangements of a kind which have already received a good deal of favourable attention from those who, for one reason or another, dislike the idea of a reconstituted open system.

In the context of our present study, the obvious starting point for an examination of alternative policies is the desire to stabilize our foreign trade, to an extent sufficient to ensure that any employment adjustments that foreign trade connections may make unavoidable shall not be on a scale larger than we can conveniently cope with. The simplest and most direct method of reducing these risks would be to reduce the normal level of our foreign imports. Something of the kind may, in any event, be necessary at least during the transitional period when the financing of imports may be unusually difficult. But however far for the sake of internal stability we might be prepared to press for a further diminution of imports, this possibility need not be considered further in detail here, where our task is to examine the structure of international trade, on the hypothesis that an open system is not attainable, but not on the hypothesis that international trade itself tends to disappear.

In an "ideal" situation, the imports which we needed would flow in to us in a steady and unbroken stream, fluctuating only to the extent to which technological progress permitted us with advantage either to replace some of them by home products, or to expand our export trade, and thus enjoy the higher standard of living which a wider range of imports would make possible for us. Theoretically, such a situation might be reached by a series of independent agreements with each of the other national economies in the world, i.e. by a strictly bilateral system in which each of our partners would guarantee a stable demand for a fraction of our exports, while in return we should be guaranteed a part of the imports which we needed. It would then be hoped that the aggregate of demands for our exports and of the imports guaranteed to us would, in each case, add up to the total which we desired. The practical complications of such a series of agreements would, however, be impossibly difficult; in any event, the "ideal" situation is almost certain to be unattainable, and as by hypothesis the primary reason for initiating any effort along these lines is a strong reluctance to form any close economic links with certain economies suspected of an abnormal propensity to fluctuation, it is more realistic to think in terms of policy which aim in the first place at closer relations with a limited number of selected partners, than of agreements intended to cover every country throughout the world.

The alternative to an open international system which has already attracted most interest, therefore, contemplates a closer integration of international trade relations within an area less extensive than the world as a whole, aiming at the canalization of the flow of trade in directions giving the best promise of stability, and maintaining only such peripheral connections as may be unavoidable with other more unstable economies outside. There are two economic criteria to be applied to determine the countries most suitable for inclusion in such a bloc. First, it would be desirable that their natural resources should be sufficiently varied and sufficiently extensive to ensure for all the members of the bloc a reasonable opportunity of securing for themselves all the goods needed for satisfactory living standards. And, secondly, there should be a high degree of uniformity in domestic policy sufficient to reduce to the minimum the risk that instability generated in one part of the area might be transmitted to other parts. The "regionalist" solution of Great Britain's post-war economic problems assumes, it has been said, the existence of "a group of countries, sufficiently complementary to one another, and sufficiently alike in their economic policies, including the pursuit of full employment, to make it easy for them to work together."[1]

The idea of such a regional economic bloc is far from being a purely academic notion. The Ottawa system of 1932 and the pre-war controlled German system are both illustrations of how it might be developed, with varied techniques, under different circumstances, and with different objectives in view. The formation of a similar bloc, the members of which were not only prepared to make the maintenance of internal stability the primary aim of their policy, but were also in substantial agreement about the means most likely to achieve this aim, is therefore not theoretically impossible. The extent to which it is worth while to spend time in examining its implications

[1] Beveridge: *Full Employment in a Free Society*, p. 239.

depends, however, mainly upon a number of practical considerations, among which the determination of possible boundaries for a workable bloc of which Great Britain would be an important if not the dominating member is perhaps the most important. In addition to the two criteria for membership already mentioned, there can be little doubt that political factors would be important in determining the countries which should or should not be closely associated in a regional economic bloc. It would be a remarkable coincidence, if the application of each of these three tests led to identical results, and conflict between their requirements would make it probable that if ever a regional bloc got going, its membership would be found not to be highly satisfactory from any one of these three points of view.

The theoretical construction of a bloc which despite these compromises might still, if nothing better was even conceivable, be described as "ideal" would, however, still be something entirely different from the practical task of selecting the most suitable members and persuading them to join the bloc. The formation of an economic bloc is not simply a matter of selecting appropriate partners, explaining to them the attractions of the offer, and promptly receiving their ready consent. Even if we could compile a list of national economies which combined a sufficient volume and variety of natural resources with a sufficient degree of uniformity in their domestic policies to make the idea of a regional bloc of which these economies would be the constituent parts attractive to us, from the point of view of British interests, there can be no certainty that the bloc could, in fact, ever be formed. Many of the elaborate statistical calculations which have sometimes been made as part of the case in favour of one form of bloc or another have little practical value, inasmuch as there is so little reason to suppose, as the architects of regional blocs are sometimes too ready to assume, that other economies will be prepared to adjust their economic activities and relations to suit our convenience, a belief which receives little support from either historical experience or theoretical analysis. Nor, if stable long-term arrangements are our objective, can much comfort

be derived from the contemplation of such temporary provisional arrangements of this kind as may already be in operation. Many economies may find it convenient to accept as a
provisional short-term measure an arrangement which would
be very distasteful as a part of their permanent economic
machinery, and in some quarters the hope has been present
that the piecemeal acceptance of these provisional measures
may create a set of vested interests sufficiently powerful ultimately to crystallize into a more permanent system. The pre-
war Schachtian drive, particularly in South-Eastern Europe,
had an objective of this kind, but that very experience itself
demonstrates the illusory character of these hopes.

We could scarcely expect the rest of the world to remain
passive spectators while we completed our negotiations with
our prospective partners. We deceive ourselves if we imagine
that after the war the leader of any proposed regional bloc can
expect to enjoy anything like the clear run which was for the
most part permitted to the Germans in the inter-war period in
building up a strong regional bloc to round off their own
inadequate natural resources. Germany, moreover, never had
to face a situation where she had to rely solely on the efficient
organization of the bloc under her control. She could always
fill in gaps and repair deficiencies by resorting to other economic
units who were not following her example. But if the regional
bloc hypothesis is now to be taken seriously, it is of little use
speculating about the shape which would be most convenient
for such a bloc under British leadership, on the assumption
that the rest of the world would carry on very much as before.
On the one hand, we must consider the probable consequences,
if we vigorously support the regional hypothesis, of a general
conviction of its value so widespread that the greater part of
the world might be organized according to this pattern. On
the other hand, it is not unlikely that the United States would
be so hostile to the regional idea as to take vigorous steps to
induce other economies under its influence to join in resisting
it. On any rational estimate of the probable advantages and
disadvantages, some economies whom we regarded as highly
suitable regional partners might therefore well prefer to stand

aloof, so that it must remain doubtful whether British invitations to join a regional bloc would elicit a number of acceptances sufficient to ensure that the bloc would be a satisfactory working proposition. The discussions in Great Britain of the Financial Agreement of December 1945 leave little doubt that considerations of this kind had a considerable influence in determining the course which the Government of the United Kingdom thought proper to recommend for the approval of Parliament. The details of the technical devices used to facilitate trade inside a regional bloc might be extremely varied, but their general purpose would be the encouragement of import demands which were expected to be fairly stable, and, at least by implication, the discouragement of demands liable to more or less violent fluctuation. It is theoretically possible, though not at all likely, that the economic integration of the various political units included in the bloc might be carried so far as to constitute a free trade area, with a degree of exchange stability as high as would be attained if the whole area had a common currency. It is more probable that the members of such a bloc would be content with an exchange of preferential advantages— from which, in the nature of things, countries outside the bloc would necessarily be excluded—and which might be made effective by a wide variety of technical devices, ranging from old-style tariff preferences, to preferential treatment in the allocation of quotas, long-term purchase agreements, with or without definite commitments for the direct exchange of exports for imports, and preferential treatment in the administration of foreign exchange controls. It is possible, though not essential for the effective working of a regional bloc, that the currencies of all its members would be freely convertible with each other without any restriction of any kind, but a greater measure of free convertibility would certainly be maintained inside the bloc than was permitted in disposing of the currencies of other countries outside. Arrangements for trade with the rest of the world would logically and necessarily be subordinated to the requirements of intra-bloc trade, while the bargaining strength of the members of the bloc would have much more influence than has hitherto been customary in determining how far the goods which importers were allowed to purchase were made to depend upon the convenience of exporting countries. Some of the regional schemes which have already been widely discussed have contemplated quite severe restrictions upon the freedom of importing countries to choose for themselves the goods which they would like to buy abroad.

The operation of these techniques raises a large number of interesting questions, both theoretical and practical, upon which there is already a considerable literature. Their further examination at this stage of our argument would, however, demand a more extended treatment than is possible without unduly expanding the limits of the present work. Whatever may be said for or against any one of these techniques—and we may repeat here that the world is unlikely in the near future to see in operation a full-blooded and thoroughly consistent open system—the practical difficulties in the way of Great Britain making them the mainstay of her commercial policy appear to be so overwhelming that any such extended treatment might fairly be criticized as a merely academic exercise.

Chapter XI

ECONOMIC AND POLITICAL IMPLICATIONS OF THE REJECTION OF AN OPEN SYSTEM

W HEN we have built up a strong critical case against a policy or set of institutions which we happen to dislike, we are often far too ready to assume, without further question, that the alternative policy or institution which we propose as a substitute will necessarily produce the desirable effects, the probable absence of which has been made the chief ground of our criticism. But though our original objections may be quite well-founded, it is equally possible that the results of the alternative course proposed may be no less disappointing, if not more so, and that the choice before us is merely one between two courses of action, either of which is likely to be embarrassing to us.

We are well advised to take very seriously the risks involved in membership of an open international economic system, but the most convincing exposition of these risks is by itself insufficient to prove that the confidence of those who believe that, both in the short run and in the long run, a regional or bilateral system will harmonize more easily with the requirements of a domestic full employment policy may not be misplaced. We are not entitled to assume that as contrasted with an open international system which would necessarily be "risky" for us, a closed regional system would be "safe". Either policy carries with it peculiar risks of its own, and there are, in any event, some substantial risks which, whatever policy we may pursue, we cannot hope to evade.

THE ECONOMIC IMPLICATIONS

The economic implications of a decision to reject an open international system and to attempt to put something different in its place may be examined from the two points of view with which we are already familiar. Would such a decision ensure better prospects for the maintenance of stable employment levels? What effects would it have upon the future course of movements in the standard of living?

If a member of an open international system wishes also to maintain full employment, it must face squarely the necessity for a continuous and never-ending series of employment adjustments, punctuated perhaps from time to time by abnormally violent adjustments in response either to a sudden change in the economic conditions of some of its more powerful partners, or to a radical technological change. The difficulty of making these adjustments may provide the strongest motive for endeavouring to avoid them, but the question whether a regional bloc would provide the insurance against instability for which we are looking still has to be examined. By rejecting an open system, and relying instead upon the operations of a regional bloc, or perhaps a number of regional blocs, the necessity for some of the smaller adjustments which would otherwise have to be made might disappear. And if our confidence in the stability of policy of the more limited circle of partners was not misplaced, some of the more extensive employment shifts, which are also often more troublesome, might also be avoided or postponed. But the stability thus apparently assured would often be merely temporary, and by postponing smaller adjustments, which otherwise we should be obliged to make with less delay, we might merely intensify the cumulative effects of the influences which made adjustment desirable, and thus render more difficult the task which sooner or later would inevitably have to be faced. In no circumstances can we get any absolute guarantee against the risks of large-scale employment shifts. All the details of a regional arrangement must necessarily be temporary. From time to time, they will have to be renewed or revised, and when revision becomes necessary— and the time-table for revision will not be determined primarily by any consideration for our own convenience—it is probable that some of the adjustments which would have been quite manageable if they had been undertaken gradually over a longer period of time will, just on account of the postponement which the specious stability of a regional arrangement will have encouraged, present an unnecessarily formidable problem.

This particular point may be most conveniently illustrated by reference to the bulk-purchase arrangements which are frequently given a prominent place in regional or bilateral programmes. At first sight, the benefits of an assured market for staple exports, which such arrangements are designed to ensure, may appear so attractive that it is not surprising that some economies who have had an unhappy experience of violently fluctuating demand for their exports are eager to enjoy them. But, in the nature of things, none of the assurances thus offered can last for ever. Sooner or later, some shift in demand or some change in the conditions of production will necessitate a revision of the terms of the original agreement, and at least one partner, and possibly both, will then be obliged to undertake a major adjustment in the structure of its employment. In an open system we get early notice of any declining trend in the demand for our exports. Under a more "orderly" system, with bilateral bargains, we are cushioned from these trends, and may not even be aware that they are taking place. In theory, the temporary stability assured might provide an opportunity for an orderly re-orientation of employment as a whole, but experience suggests that it is much more likely to be thankfully accepted as an excuse for doing little or nothing. In the interval, competitors may get a lead in supplying new types of goods which subsequently we are never able to overtake. Even if we accept stability as the primary objective of our policy, we might therefore wisely hesitate before committing ourselves to a system of international trade, which, whatever its immediate attractions, is certain from time to time to subject us to some very awkward jolts.

These risks are naturally greater for the smaller and weaker economies, who will usually be in a relatively weak bargaining position for making bilateral agreements or for establishing a satisfactory position for themselves inside a regional bloc, and it is no accident that the initiative in these arrangements has usually come from the larger and stronger powers. Small economies can have little hope of checking or controlling world trends, and the most sensible course for them is the speediest possible adaptation. But it is easy to exaggerate the extent to which even a large and powerful economy can, in the long run, count on getting the protection which regional arrangements seem to offer. We have already seen that much of the prestige which the idea of regionalism at present enjoys in many quarters, is based on a misinterpretation of the "success" of German policy during the inter-war period. Germany's partners in that venture were, for the most part, victims of shock tactics. Taken by surprise in a world which offered them few satisfactory alternatives, there was no other course effectively open to them but to accept the German invitation. But though the immediate damage inflicted upon their economic structure has sometimes been exaggerated, none of the partners were happy in the association which had been forced upon them, and this not merely on account of its unfavourable political implications. Already before the war they were struggling, within the limits of their power, to free themselves from the unwelcome bonds which they had been obliged to accept, and there was some evidence that their efforts were meeting with a certain amount of success. It is not now very profitable to speculate on what might have happened had war not broken out, but there is some significance in the fact that the Germans felt obliged to follow up their early measures of economic control by political and military domination.

Not only the terms of a regional arrangement, but also the membership of a regional bloc may also need revision from time to time. The interests of members will inevitably change, and it is by no means inconceivable that a country which at one time was prepared to enter a regional bloc, would later decide that for it the balance of advantages was on the side of withdrawal. The stability of a regional bloc whose membership thus changed from time to time could not be very great. In 1932, Canada was perhaps the most ardent of the Dominions in pressing for the extension of imperial preference. To-day, partly as a result of experience of the working of the Ottawa Agreements, but partly also on account of changes in the structure of the Canadian economy which had already begun before the war, and have been considerably accelerated by the demands of a war economy, Canada's enthusiasm for the Ottawa system has become quite lukewarm, and the Canadian Government is anxious to assist the United Kingdom in freeing itself from the restrictions of regionalism. Similar changes, both of national interest and of public opinion, may be expected in the future, so that any hopes that the world might now once and for all be carved up in a neat framework of regional blocs are unlikely to be well founded. Theoretical analyses of economic regionalism tend, moreover, to take it for granted that there will be no great practical difficulty in satisfying the import demands of all the partners. But one can frequently detect a tendency to ride roughshod over the uncontrolled preferences of consumers, and to assume that the smaller economies must, within limits, be prepared just to take what the more powerful economies find it convenient to let them have. Especially if they are temporarily in peculiar difficulties, the smaller economies may be prepared to accept such a position if any alternative immediately available threatens to be even worse. But it can scarcely be claimed that arrangements of this kind justify any firm expectation of permanent stability. Sooner or later the time will come when temporary difficulties will disappear, or at least be modified to such an extent that the smaller economies will no longer feel obliged to defer to the wishes of a single powerful partner, and when that time comes, regional blocs are likely to be most unstable.

There are, therefore, good reasons for doubting whether the substitution of a series of regional blocs for a new open international system, which seems so risky from the point of view of internal stability, would, in fact, except perhaps for quite a short period, produce the expected result. Some troublesome employment adjustments might be avoided, but others, no less troublesome, would soon take their place. There remain to be considered the probable effects of regionalism upon standards of living. The analysis of this point is necessarily more speculative, but even if we take the most optimistic view of future developments, it confirms the view that, especially for the

United Kingdom, the risks of regionalism are at best no less than the risks of an open international system.

THE THEORY OF "PRODUCTIVE AUTARCHY"

We have already referred (in Chapter V) to the view that recent technological progress has now brought the world to such a stage in its evolution, that any further benefits likely to accrue from maintaining or extending the existing patterns of international division of labour will soon be negligible as compared with the benefits to be enjoyed if suitably equipped regional blocs progressively limit their economic entanglements with the rest of the world, and concentrate instead upon control of their own internal policies with little concern for the vagaries of other economies elsewhere. This view has been widely held, and its influence is not a new element in the international situation. After the Great Depression, when American policy was being severely criticized as a disruptive factor, many Americans were disposed to turn the tables upon their critics by arguing that "the major portion of the disturbances to our internal peace and prosperity, have their origin in forces working from the outside through our foreign trade and our foreign exchanges". "Science", it was affirmed, "has destroyed the basis for the larger part of international trade and therefore the basis of the old internationalism, based on free trade", and Americans were invited to face the question "whether the United States will take the opportunity which is offered, to shape her own life in her own way and in accord with her own ideals, or whether this opportunity will be thrust aside for an elusive and delusive old-world concept of sordid international shopkeeping."[1] The background within which similar ideas are now presented has changed a little, but their essential content remains much the same.

The history of the effects of technological change upon international trade is a subject to which much more attention might profitably be paid. It has sometimes compelled a revolutionary re-orientation of customary trade channels, as, for example, when the development of synthetic nitrates disrupted

[1] Crowther, *America Self-Contained*, pp. 336-7, 10, 4-5.

the economy of Chile. Even a superficial survey, however, suggests the great difficulty of formulating any confident or reliable generalizations upon the subject. Some technological improvements have greatly increased the dependence of the more advanced industrial countries upon raw materials and fuel supplies, which could only be obtained in adequate quantities from other countries, or have in other directions widened the range within which international division of labour afforded further opportunities for raising standards of living. Other technological changes have facilitated the economic exploitation of home supplies, and therefore diminished dependence on international trade. Sometimes and for some countries, changes of the first type have been the more important, but at other times and in other places the second has predominated. It may be true that "the standard of living which could be maintained with no trade or little trade, is higher than it was thirty years ago. But it does not follow that the improvement in that standard which can be secured by utilizing to the full international division of labour is less than it was. If the national income which can be produced without the help of foreign trade has been raised by the advance in the 'synthetic industries', the volume of production which can be obtained with the help of trade has also been pushed up."[1]

The future is certain to produce many more changes of both kinds, and it is impossible to predict with confidence that either type is certain to outweigh the other. The view which we are now criticizing assumes that the balance will be strongly tipped in favour of the second group of influences. The raw materials likely to have the greatest significance in the new chemical and other industries of the future, it is argued, will probably be more or less abundantly available in all parts of the world, the opportunities will steadily expand for satisfying our needs by applying chemical processes to "local sawdust and mud",[2] so that the cost differentials between producers

---

[1] G. Haberler, "Some Factors affecting International Trade and International Economic Policy", in *Economic Reconstruction*, ed. Seymour E. Harris, p. 321.

[2] D. H. Robertson, "The Future of International Trade", *Economic Journal*, March 1938, p. 12.

in one country and another will tend to narrow and ultimately to disappear.

In certain industries, no doubt, such a tendency will make itself felt. But even if its influence were likely to be very far-reaching, we should not be justified in relegating the benefits of a world-wide division of labour to the subordinate place which those who emphasize this view would assign to it. Many of the processes of production which modern technological trends make possible are extremely complicated, and their probable effects upon international trade must be judged in the light not only of the demand for the traditional basic raw materials, but also of the continuing and perhaps increasing necessity for combining with the newer raw materials small but quite essential quantities of other productive factors which cannot be obtained at home, and which, in some cases, had little relevance to the older production processes now being displaced, and therefore played little part in international trade. Improvements in transport, affecting both the speed and the cost of moving goods, and in particular widening the range within which perishable commodities can be economically distributed, have historically been among the most significant technological factors in international trade, and we are still very far from seeing the end of scientific progress in this field. In the future, as in the past, improvements in transport may well bring within the normal range of international trade goods whose distribution had formerly been inevitably highly localized. There is nothing in the character of modern technological change to rule out the possibility that some countries may, in the future, find it highly advantageous to import some goods which at present have little or no place in their foreign trade. The only generalization which can safely be made is that the effect of technological change upon the place of international trade in our economic life is likely to be ambivalent, working simultaneously in both directions.

The practical conclusions to be drawn from this analysis would be no different even if it could be conclusively proved that the technological changes of the future would inevitably diminish the statistical importance of international trade as compared with national income. In discussing the special case of Great Britain, we have already seen that the statistical ratio of foreign trade to national income has less significance than the actual content of the goods imported. It would be quite conceivable that the ratio should decline at the same time as foreign trade became more essential—if it is permissible to talk about degrees of essentiality.

Technological change may affect the content of the imports likely to be beneficial to our standard of living, not only because of its effects upon our productive capacity, but also because of changes in our demand, arising from those very improvements in standards of living which technological change should make possible. If standards of living are to rise, the pattern of international trade should be adjusted to the new demands which could then become effective. Many of these demands could most conveniently be satisfied by the purchase of goods from countries or regions other than that in which the purchaser was living, so that the net effects upon international trade should again, as has so often happened in the past, be described in terms of a shift from one type of import to another, rather than an absolute decline in their aggregate volume. This point has special importance for Great Britain, whose "natural" competitive advantages in international trade are likely to be more and more concentrated in the production of goods, attractive mainly to people with relatively high incomes.

The importance of these considerations is in no way diminished by the fact that, as incomes rise, there is sure to be a steady growth in the importance of services as elements in real income, and that as the largest proportion of services must necessarily be produced at home, we might on this account, therefore, in any case expect the statistical importance of international trade, which is largely, though not exclusively, an exchange of goods, to decline. We may note in passing, indeed, that the significance of services for international trade might, in suitable circumstances in the future, become much greater than in the past; the more important point, however, is that to which attention has already been drawn, that statistical calculations of the ratio of imports to national income have less significance than the extent to which imports provide part of the essential structure without which the other elements in real income may fail to materialize.

In any event, even if the trend were clear and unambiguous, there is no convincing reason why we should hastily anticipate its results. "Why should the fact that the scope for advantageous exchange between nations is narrowing be an argument for putting increased obstacles in the way of such exchange as still remains advantageous?"[1] We should adapt the economic policy of to-day to the conditions of to-day, rather than to the hypothetical conditions of twenty or thirty years hence.

THE INTERESTS OF GREAT BRITAIN

The discussion of this question has so far been conducted in quite general terms. There are, however, some additional factors of special interest for the peculiar conditions of Great Britain. Even if it could be shown that, in the long run, there was a good prospect either for single countries or for regional blocs so to develop synthetic products as to diminish progressively and permanently the value for them of outside trade connections, it would nevertheless be most embarrassing for Great Britain if this doctrine were to be precipitately or widely applied at the present time. The United States is probably the one country which could make the adjustments necessary for autarchy with speed and with the least possible inconvenience to its people. The inconveniences should not be minimized, but they would not be insuperable. It would, however, be extremely awkward for Great Britain (and indeed for many other countries) if the United States were to begin to apply the doctrine systematically and seriously, before the rest of the world was ready for it. Even the most optimistic would not care in the immediate future to base economic policy exclusively upon the doctrine of "productive autarchy". There are everywhere certain important transitional adjustments which ought to be made first. Everybody needs aid from the United States, directly or indirectly, for economic recovery and reconstruction, and if United States policy was too promptly

[1] Robertson, loc. cit., p. 8.

adjusted to the view that international trade was declining in importance, this aid would be cut off, or at best reduced to such modest proportions that post-war adjustments would be seriously retarded. We cannot begin to practise the doctrine of "productive autarchy" until a more or less stable set of conditions has been established, from which the movement towards autarchy could proceed in a more or less orderly manner. Such conditions do not exist at the present time, and are unlikely to be present for a long time to come. Any hasty adoption of the doctrine might indefinitely postpone the date of their appearance.

No one, indeed, has ever seriously suggested that Great Britain should ever attempt to practise a policy of "productive autarchy" based upon nothing but her own resources. It is always assumed that she will enjoy the co-operation of complementary partners. But even if the most favourable hypothesis of this kind were realized, Great Britain would still be in a peculiarly difficult situation for maintaining an adequate volume of "essential" supplies of goods which she could not herself conveniently produce.

We have already had occasion to refer to the unique position which imports occupy in the structure of the British economy.[1] It is significant that even during the war, when many imports for ordinary civilian use practically disappeared, the contraction in the volume of our imports was much less than might have been expected. Excluding munitions, United Kingdom imports still in 1942 amounted to as much as 72 per cent of the 1938 total, and in 1943 to 79 per cent.[2] The consequences of the disappearance of a very small fraction of British imports might be borne with equanimity, but if the fraction expanded beyond this limit, the effects upon standards of living might be catastrophic, even though arithmetically it might still not appear very formidable.

It has, indeed, been argued that while it is unlikely that "we can reduce our imports to the extent needed to bridge the anticipated gap in our international accounts without affecting

[1] Cf. Chapter VIII, pp. 119-20.
[2] Statistics Relating to the War Effort of the United Kingdom, Cmd. 6564, 1944, p. 45.

the standard of life", it is nevertheless probable that "a 10 per cent contraction of imports (which would make as big a contribution as an 18 per cent expansion of exports) would be easier to effect and need not involve any very great or lasting hardship."[1] But even if this rather optimistic view were accepted, it would have little practical significance in relation to contractions of imports on the larger scale, which in certain circumstances might be imposed upon us if an adequate international system failed to materialize, and which therefore cannot be dismissed as a mere academic speculation. And it must also be recalled that the problems of full employment and of international trade are closely connected mainly because it is anticipated that a high level of employment would raise the normal level of our import requirements. To that extent the thesis that "the maintenance of the standard of life of the population depends much more on maintaining full employment (in the economy as a whole) than on fractional changes in imports or exports"[2] is misleading, inasmuch as it implies an unreal choice between two alternative lines of action. Any favourable effects which full employment might have upon the British standard of living will not be fully realized if the necessary imports are not forthcoming. It would be going too far to say that for us it is a case of All or Nothing, but it is difficult to discover any half-way house for the British economy between the maintenance of a standard of living not very much below the pre-war level and a quite catastrophic decline.

Any estimate of the probable extent of the damage likely to be inflicted upon British standards of living, if the failure to reconstruct a world-wide international economic system seriously narrowed the range of markets from which we could draw our imports, must necessarily be speculative. A good deal will depend upon the consequences, immediate and remote, beneficial or otherwise, for the British economy of the technical changes which have been stimulated by the activities of the war, and these we cannot at the moment confidently forecast. In agriculture in particular, extensive claims have been made of

[1] Henry Clay, "The Place of Exports in British Industry after the War", *Economic Journal*, June-September 1942, p. 151.
[2] Henry Clay, loc. cit., p. 151.

great increases in efficiency which, even on narrowly economic grounds, may justify a substantial reduction in the degree of our dependence upon overseas food supplies, and these claims are not to be lightly set aside, though they would command more confidence if those who make them were to show themselves more ready to dispense with protective props.

Provided that we remember that changes in the basic conditions of production may render irrelevant any hasty conclusions drawn from the experience of the past, we may, however, form a useful if rough picture of the significance for British standards of living of membership of a world-wide economic system by examining the character of our imports before the war. This examination suggests that, unless there are very far-reaching changes in the structure of British production, extending a good deal further than most people have so far cared to contemplate, any failure to maintain our imports at something near their customary level would damage our standards of living to quite an appreciable extent, and that in such circumstances, the maintenance of full employment in this country could not assure the standards of living which many take for granted.

In value, Great Britain's imports between 1936 and 1938 averaged £866 millions per annum. Of this, foodstuffs, drink and tobacco accounted for over £402 millions, raw materials for nearly £237 millions, and manufactured goods, including semi-manufactures, for about £221½ millions. Each of these groups included a wide variety of items, but a more detailed investigation of the more important items[1] shows the scope for cuts in imports which would not inflict perceptible damage upon our standard of living to be quite restricted. During the war, the comparative importance of British home-grown food has substantially increased, but even if the most favourable view is taken of our war-time food standards, our war-time experience has shown us that without radical and far-reaching changes in British agricultural production, an appreciable contraction in the volume of our food imports would involve

[1] cf. G. D. H. Cole, *Great Britain in the Post-War World*, London, Gollancz, 1942, pp. 31-35, 39-46.

a highly inconvenient decline in our standards of living. Imports of raw materials are even more "essential" for the maintenance of satisfactory employment levels, "for British industries are heavily dependent on imported materials which cannot be produced at home", while a large proportion of the imports of manufactured goods are no less essential than raw materials for the maintenance of normal levels of industrial production.

The question which here chiefly concerns us is whether by entrusting our fortunes to bilateral or regional bloc exchanges we would in the difficult situation which in any event now confronts us have a better chance of getting the imports we need than by participating whole-heartedly in an open international system. For a conclusive and final answer to this question, we should have to embark upon a much more detailed and elaborate analysis than is possible here. But especially when we recall the difficulties already mentioned of ensuring that the partners who would be most useful to us would whole-heartedly collaborate with us, we can scarcely resist the conclusion that our best hope should be centred in a broadly based open international system.

To arguments of this kind it is sometimes urged in reply, that no one seriously contemplates a complete break in all our economic links with the United States. This very plea, however, thoroughly justified though it may be, in fact strengthens the argument for accepting the risks involved in membership of an open system. Most of these risks are rooted in our fears that a too close association with the volatile Americans will impose upon us more violent economic fluctuations than we care to face. But these risks will still remain, unless we are prepared to reduce our connections with the United States to the barest minimum. The value of any protection to be gained by limiting our connections should be estimated by comparison not only with the risks of damaging counter-attacks, but also with the residue of normal risks of fluctuations generated in the United States, which would still inevitably remain so long as we found it necessary to preserve any substantial connections with that economy. By too cautiously limiting the range of our connections, without ever being prepared to go the whole hog, we might easily find that in the end we had made sure of getting the worst of both worlds.

If our international situation should become really desperate, it would certainly be unfair to place the whole responsibility for the lower standards of living which we might be compelled to accept upon any full employment policy which we might decide to adopt. But if our reluctance to use such influence as we had in favour of the restoration of an open system was, to any significant extent, based upon our preference for one particular type of full employment policy, our critics might justifiably claim that the austerity to which we found ourselves condemned had been deepened by our pre-occupation with full employment in that sense. In any event, we are obliged to face uncertainties. But the evils likely to arise from the un-certainties of bilateralism and regionalism are measurably greater than the uncertainties of an open international system.

We have already referred to the dangerous delusion that whatever decisions we may think it proper to make in deter-mining our own policy, we can count on other countries continuing to behave just as before. Especially in a case where strong passions can easily be aroused, any such confidence is unjustified. In more specific terms, we may say that while it is impossible to predict in detail what the United States would have done if confronted with a decision on our part not to implement the obligations of Article VII, it would certainly have done something, and almost certainly something damaging to British interests. The objections to "discrimination" are so strongly held in that country that any decision to incorporate as permanent parts of our trade structure measures which could plausibly be so described would provoke considerable resentment, and resentment, moreover, which would not be allayed by any demonstration that inconsistencies or contra-dictions could be detected in any definition of discrimination. This is, indeed, one good reason for doubting whether the discussion of the economics of regional blocs may not be merely academic, in the bad sense of that term. If the knowledge that United States reactions would be hostile deterred some economies whose participation was vital from joining a bloc of the kind in which Great Britain was interested, their unwillingness to co-operate would deprive the idea of anything but theoretical interest.

The United States is not in a favourable position itself to practise the techniques which have been developed as characteristic of the modern regional bloc. But these techniques do not exhaust the range of possibilities whereby the policies of other countries may be influenced. The very wealth of the United States makes it possible to contemplate seriously the extension of subsidized exports on a very large scale, as well as the granting of capital loans on terms which might be very damaging to Great Britain. It is not necessary here to elaborate in great detail the weapons in the armoury of economic warfare which would be available to the United States, but in forming a final judgment about our own future international economic policy, we should take into account the important fact that such weapons exist and that some of them have an uncomfortably keen edge. The world as a whole, and we in Great Britain in particular, would obviously be much poorer if the American continent were suddenly to disappear, but our position in that catastrophic event might be quite favourable as compared with what it would be in a world where the United States felt itself justified in adopting a policy of retaliation against us.

It has been argued that "the threat of retaliation against policies which are 'discriminatory' only in so far as it is necessary to maintain full employment in the countries practising it is akin to the behaviour of the dog in the manger. It would be a different matter if foreign trade controls and bilateral agreements were used for the purpose of enforcing more favourable terms of trade against the 'free' market countries."[1] In practice, however, it is to be feared, this distinction will not easily be drawn, and what is perhaps of still greater practical importance, any distinction which we affirm can properly be drawn is unlikely to commend itself to those against whom we are discriminating. It would be a poor consolation if we had nothing

[1] T. Balogh, "A Note on the Economics of Retaliation", *Review of Economic Studies*, Summer 1944, p. 86.

to offset the losses which retaliation would inflict upon us, except protestations of injured innocence which other people failed to find convincing.

THE POLITICAL IMPLICATIONS

There remain to be considered the political implications of a decision to reject the open system. On this issue an economist is no more entitled to be heard than any other citizen who has given the pros and cons such careful consideration as he can. But especially at the present time, when it is being more and more generally recognized that both economic and political factors must be taken into account in seeking for satisfactory answers to difficult questions, it would be foolish to pursue a purely economic analysis without constantly bearing this intimate relation in mind. Theoretically, one might picture a world in which the political and economic relations of the more important states were determined quite independently of each other, the closest political relations being compatible with the most complete lack of co-ordination of economic policy. Whatever the difficulties of the future relations between the United States and the U.S.S.R., no one believes that they cannot be friendly because there is every prospect that the economic policies of these two countries will continue for a long time to develop on quite different lines. But divergence in this case does not necessarily imply conflict, and to imagine that satisfactory Anglo-American political relations could be maintained after a head-on collision in the economic field, which to many Americans would seem to imply a wanton disregard for the obligations imposed by Article VII of the Lend-Lease Agreement, pre-supposes a much higher degree of optimism than can rationally be justified. It would, no doubt, be wrong invariably to make decisions on economic policy depend upon over-riding political considerations, but especially when we bear in mind the highly dubious economic consequences of the rejection of an open system, we are entitled to regard the political consequences as a further factor necessitating the greatest caution before any irrevocable step of this kind is taken.

Chapter XII

CONCLUSION

ANYONE who embarked upon a study of the kind which we have here undertaken in the expectation that at its conclusion he would be able to present a series of neat and definite conclusions, would certainly be disappointed, and no apology is needed because our analysis has not revealed anything of the kind. The problems with which we have been dealing are complex to an unusual degree, and even if decisions which appear at the time to be irrevocable are taken in regard to any one of them, continual adaptations of policy will always be needed in the light of changes in the background which by their very nature are at present unpredictable. In an important sense, therefore, none of our problems can ever be finally and completely solved. Indeed, if there is one certain moral which emerges from our inquiry, it is that the practical issue is always that of balancing one set of risks against another.

The present study was initiated many months before the announcement of the Financial Agreement between the United States and the United Kingdom in December 1945,[1] and at a less advanced stage of the negotiations from which that Agreement emerged, our conclusions would naturally have been presented in a somewhat different form. In one important sense the issue is now, at least for the time being, officially determined. The Government of the United Kingdom was already formally committed to collaborate in the re-establishment of a new open international economic system in a world much more determined than its predecessors to maintain high and stable levels of employment, but the Financial Agreement and the accompanying documents carry it a stage further by purporting to provide the concrete conditions required if this commitment is to be translated into positive acts of policy. In the current debates, especially in Great Britain, it is true that the issue of full employment has not taken that central

[1] Cmd. 6708.

place in the picture which is properly accorded to it in an analysis which sets out to answer the questions which we put to ourselves at the beginning of this study. Many of the motives and feelings which have influenced opinion have, indeed, been much more concerned with matters outside the range of our present investigation, and upon which, therefore, no judgment need be pronounced here; in particular, the immediate and pressing difficulties of the British economy, to which we have several times referred, have naturally impressed themselves upon the public mind much more than any fears of repercussions upon full employment policy which are still a matter for the future. Nevertheless, while a full examination of all the implications and ramifications of the Financial Agreement and the understandings and obligations associated with it is not called for in the present context, its terms are clearly highly relevant to the longer range considerations which we have been discussing.

The general tenor of our argument has been definitely in favour of accepting the risks necessarily associated with the Agreement. There will naturally still be sharp differences of opinion as to how far the guarantees already provided, or still in contemplation, add up to anything which a prudent British statesman would be justified in regarding as an adequate "safeguard" for his country, or for the internal policies to which it is equally committed. But when we take into account all the other considerations to which attention has been directed, when we bear in mind the dubious consequences of any alternative course which we might have thought of following, and especially if we are firmly resolved not to permit any further dangerous delays in grappling with all the other important and closely inter-related international issues upon which the future course of the evolution of our economy depends, we should probably feel obliged to support him as he decided to take the plunge and face the risks involved, lest something much worse should befall. The conditions of human society seldom make it possible to find a firm basis for action on the principle that we should "make no commitment of any kind, except in return for solid advantages which we know will be lasting and enduring."[1] "Those who say that they are prepared to come to agreements with other countries, but only upon the basis that we get our own way on every topic, or that their own particular theoretical convictions are completely safeguarded, are in effect saying that they are not prepared to enter into international agreements at all."[2] Great Britain to-day is certainly not, and probably never will be, in such a position as would justify us in refusing to undertake the obligations of international agreements except on such terms.

Few would defend the thesis that membership of an open system may not on occasion place us in an awkward situation. We have been perfectly justified in pressing for such safeguards as we could get; there are, moreover, still a number of important undecided issues to be further discussed at the International Conference on Trade and Employment to be summoned early in 1947, and there will be equal justification for continuing to press there for further safeguards. But it should be clearly understood from the outset that in a highly imperfect world it is quite impossible to get anything like all the safeguards that would please us. Both general processes of reasoning and an examination of the peculiar position and problems of the British economy combine, however, to establish the conclusion that the re-establishment of an open international order is, in the long run, such an overwhelmingly powerful British interest that we should make every effort to ensure that it will work, even if in so doing we are obliged to face certain risks which we should have preferred to avoid.

It has already been pointed out that while we are filling in the details of our formal picture of the structure and implications of an open international system, we should not forget that we are quite unlikely for some time to come to get anything which corresponds exactly with our more optimistic hopes. We must certainly be prepared for inconsistencies and unevennesses, and they will probably not be confined to the immediate period of transition when every one is already more or less reconciled to their inevitability. On the other hand, while the

[1] Viscount Swinton, in the House of Lords, December 18, 1945, Parliamentary Debates (Lords), Vol. 138, Col. 797.

[2] Sir Stafford Cripps, in the House of Commons, December 12, 1945, Parliamentary Debates (Commons), Vol. 417, Col. 482.

acceptance of an open system in no way obliges us to abandon or even seriously to modify our interest in a high level of employment as an overriding objective of national policy, we should also be prepared for some compromises in that field too. We are committed in Great Britain to the most vigorous efforts to construct social security machinery on a scale and administered on principles of which a genuinely civilized society need not be ashamed, for we believe that the innocent victims of social and economic change should, without loss of dignity or self-respect, be safeguarded against being sacrificed in the interests of the general convenience. It is, on the face of it, at first sight a little paradoxical that so many of us should at the same time be at least equally insistent that it will be something like a social disgrace if, apart from a few trifling marginal cases, the machinery ever has to be used. There is indeed, every reason why we should not complacently accept the machinery of social insurance as an excuse for inaction or dilatoriness in dealing with the remediable fundamental causes of the misfortunes against which insurance is being provided. If, however, employment is to be interpreted strictly as meaning active participation in production, it is worth while to recall that an individual often finds it not only convenient but necessary to vary the tempo of his work from time to time, to such an extent indeed that, provided that the continuity of his income is not thereby impaired, periods during which productive activity is entirely suspended may be very welcome to him. There are good reasons for believing that, in this instance, the analogy between the life of an individual and the life of a society is a good one, and that in a condition of healthy economic development there will, from time to time, be fluctuations in the volume and intensity of economic activity which may properly be reflected in parallel fluctuations in the statistics of employment. If this view is sound, there is much to be said for straightforwardly accepting the fact, and refraining from an undue straining after continuity of employment for its own sake. There can be no justification for chronic depression or mass unemployment; interruptions in employment are, however, a social evil mainly because of the interruptions of income which have hitherto been their normal accompaniment and of the uncertainty of their duration. If socially undesirable income fluctuations could be avoided, or their consequences effectively mitigated, we might be justified at certain stages of economic development in regarding fluctuations in active employment a good deal wider than are contemplated in some of the current definitions of full employment, as not only unavoidable in a changing world, but actually as in the general interest, and, therefore, also in insisting that those who were not engaged in active productive work should not necessarily on that account be held to be socially inferior or subjected to severe financial embarrassment.

Many suggestions have been made relating to the issues here raised, a full examination of which would, however, lead us far beyond the proper limits of the present study. It might, for example, be profitable to inquire how far the practice of relatively long-term contracts of employment might with advantage be extended. Historical accidents have played a part in determining the fields of employment where the benefits of this practice are enjoyed to-day, and there is no obvious justification for the view that in all other occupations and industries it would be entirely unsuitable. It would, indeed, be simpleminded to imagine that all the complex problems of unemployment could be neatly solved at one stroke by what, in effect, would be a far-reaching extension of the custom of holidays on full pay. Much of our thinking about unemployment would, however, be clearer and more fruitful if we could resolutely abjure the natural but unfortunate habit of thinking in terms of some hypothetical simple omnibus solution which will cover every conceivable instance. No such solution exists; the idea of extending the practice of long-term contracts of employment is mentioned here merely as an illustration, possibly not in itself very important, but still not entirely negligible, of a wide variety of measures which, taken together, might provide something that we need not be embarrassed to describe as a "solution" of the problem.

Leaving details aside, however, the important point is that we should not form the habit of regarding any failure on our part to maintain, as a normal practice, Sir William Beveridge's low standard of 3 per cent of unemployed as due mainly or merely to the ignorance and prejudice of other countries with whom we are obliged, however reluctantly, to maintain close economic connections. In a resilient and vigorously expanding economy, it might often properly be regarded rather as the normal accompaniment of economic changes which it was one of the main purposes of the economy to facilitate and accelerate; provided that at the same time proper protection was afforded against the risks of income fluctuation—and a resilient and vigorously expanding economy need not find that a very troublesome business—we need not feel ashamed of ourselves if at any point of time we should find that the proportion of the labour force which was not engaged in active and productive work had risen above 3 per cent.

In the international field the practical conclusion readily drawn by any observer in the United Kingdom is the overwhelming importance of United States policy as a factor determining the course of development of the new international order. The maintenance in the United States of a level of general demand high enough to generate a demand for imports of sufficient volume to enable other countries to discharge their obligations, and the relaxation of the restrictions which have hitherto cramped the United States demand for imports even when the general level of demand in that country was adequate, are both matters of the most direct concern for the smooth working of this order. To what extent United States policy in these fields will display the boldness and farsightedness which is as much in her own interest as in that of the rest of the world, is a question to which no final answer has yet been given, or perhaps can ever be given, if final is interpreted as meaning decisions never again to be questioned until the end of time. It is a sobering truth that all of us will be in a bad way if the United States fails to maintain a reasonably stable level of employment, and if there is no reform, going much further than mere formal change, of the traditional United States restrictive foreign trade policy. But we certainly do ourselves no good, and may conceivably do much harm, by in effect telling the Americans beforehand that we have no confidence in either their capacity or their willingness to grapple with either of these issues, and gloating in anticipation over the mess into which the more gloomy of our prophets see them landing both themselves and the rest of the world.

In any event, while he may be excused for taking a lively interest in the decisions to be made in other economies, which on any hypothesis are certain to have the most direct bearing upon his own welfare, the observer in the United Kingdom will be still more profitably engaged in looking about for morals which he can apply to himself and to his own country. In the course of our analysis we have repeatedly returned to the underlying theme of the importance of the highest possible degree of flexibility in our economic structure. Unless this is assured the conflict between stable employment and rising standards of living, which would otherwise be a merely theoretical possibility, could easily become a most unpleasant reality. Economies and industries outside our own borders which have formed a sturdy habit of quickly adjusting their structure to changes in the technique of production or in the demands of their customers will be less tempted to press for the imposition of restrictive policies which would damage both our standards of living and our level of employment, and if we could count on this habit as an automatic reaction throughout our own commerce and industry, we ourselves would be in a much more favourable position for facing the inevitable changes and chances of a difficult world. It has become a commonplace to insist upon the favourable bargaining position conferred upon Great Britain by its status as "the world's best customer". But the permanent bargaining strength of a customer cannot be very great if he, whether deliberately or not, creates the impression that he has neither the intention nor the capacity to provide those with whom he does business with the goods which they want to buy. It may be unfair to suggest that this impression accurately reflects the state of mind of many, or perhaps of any, of those who have been most critical of the Financial Agreement. It is not, however, open to doubt that the tone of the public discussion in certain quarters of the future of British commercial policy has, fairly or unfairly, left an impression of this kind in the minds of many observers outside this country, and it is a matter of the most urgent necessity to take vigorous steps to dispel it. Curiously enough, in view of the widespread belief in Great Britain that an important American motive in pressing the present proposals is an eager desire to establish the American competitive position as quickly as possible on the firmest possible foundations, there is nothing which would be more effective in establishing and maintaining the prestige of this country, both in the United States and elsewhere, than convincing evidence that we were aware of the overwhelming importance of efficiency throughout our industry and were already engaged in active steps to raise our standards to the highest possible level. Even the best that we can do in this field will not, of course, make the path of the British economy easy during the next few years. But action based upon such motives as these would serve the double purpose of mitigating some of the difficulties which in any event have to be faced, and of establishing our reputation throughout the world as a people prepared to contribute its utmost to the general task of reconstruction and development, instead of timidly drawing back within a privileged circle where we hoped, rather too optimistically, that we might be accorded a favoured position justified by our own interpretation of our past achievements.

Unfortunately, or perhaps fortunately, a policy founded upon such considerations as these offers little suitable material for stirring slogans. Even the most eloquent speeches on the subject are unconvincing unless they are accompanied by positive action, and in the nature of things very little of the action can have the character of drama. If, however, it is along these lines that our thoughts would be most profitably directed, whichever purpose among our tangled complex of objectives happens to arouse our livelier personal interest and enthusiasm, our analysis of the inter-relations between full employment policy and the implications of an open international economic system may properly be brought to a conclusion on this note.

A COMMENT

CERTAIN members of the Group which has discussed the problems treated in this volume wish to add a comment. Its purpose is not to dissent from the arguments used or conclusions reached by Professor Fisher, which are in their judgment important and correct, but only to give a somewhat different emphasis in regard to one particular topic.

Professor Fisher has considered the arguments for and against a policy of open international trading relations. His decisive verdict is that such a policy would best suit the interests of this country. His arguments appear cogent and unanswerable. This review is surely most timely. Public opinion has recently been hesitant and oscillating; in the overcharged atmosphere of the drama through which we have been living, its mood has been such as to shirk a thoroughgoing re-examination of fundamentals. No writer of eminence has reviewed the question as a whole. Isolated arguments have been put forward for possible advantages to be derived from a system of bilateral bargaining, and the impact of those upon the public mind in its present weak and convalescent condition has been out of proportion to their intrinsic value. Men are left wondering and not a little bewildered. This volume with its steady, unimpassioned and comprehensive treatment should be a valuable restorative. A strong case is made that the principal arguments for the traditional British commercial policy still hold in modern conditions, and on the basis of this case anxious doubters may reasonably set their minds at rest.

Professor Fisher has argued mainly from the standpoint of British interests. Reasonings based on more altruistic considerations would not have eased the doubts of those who have regard to the present parlous state of the country nor have impressed the foreigner ready to pick up the scent of hypocrisy. None the less, it may be consoling to those in whom some flame of idealism still burns, albeit weakly in the inclement world

192

of to-day, that the welfare of mankind will also be advanced by the policy recommended.

Intertwined with this question of foreign trade policy are arguments relating to the crucial importance of adaptability and willingness to accept adjustments in our economic system. Professor Fisher stresses the point that the claim for "full" employment must not be taken to abrogate the claim for a decent and improving standard of living. Our people would by no means be content with full employment at Victorian wages. They hope for improvement even by comparison with the inter-war period. But this cannot be achieved unless we remain constantly ready to make changes. Now a change implies not only that some one must begin producing something that was not produced before, or using a method of production that was not used before, but also that some one, and, indeed, many thousands of people, and, if we look at the world as a whole, perhaps many millions of people, must cease doing what they have been doing before.

Under an open foreign trade system the need for such adjustments becomes evident at once; under a closed system it may be possible to defer them. If we defer them, our standard of living certainly suffers; but it is not clear that in the long run we really gain anything on the side of reducing the need for adjustment. An adjustment deferred is an adjustment all the same. If all adjustments are deferred our standard of living is continuously lower than it might be, but there is no less adjustment in the end—unless as a price for stationariness we are prepared to suffer progressive and mounting losses.

Thus external policy and the need to be adaptable are linked. But Professor Fisher clearly also feels that current ideas and enthusiasms in regard to a domestic policy for "full" employment have dangers in this connection. Do they not, on the face of them, militate against the objective of wresting large numbers of people from their traditional work? Do they not encourage the idea that people have some sort of right to expect to be left in employment in their present occupation? This stress which Professor Fisher lays on the danger that current ideas may encourage the shoring up of unsound structures, the maintenance of employment in specific trades or industries at a given level regardless of economic requirement, is also timely and important. Plans implying such a point of view or having such a consequence should be ruthlessly rejected.

In his anxiety to expose this danger, however, Professor Fisher may give the impression of seeming to belittle the "full" employment problem in a way that he does not intend and, possibly, may in his own mind attach less importance to it than in our judgment should be attached. We are adding this note to make it plain that the arguments and conclusions of this volume do not, in our opinion, at all tend to invalidate the two following propositions.

The first is that it is a responsibility of society to secure that large scale unemployment does not develop. This is recognized in the White Paper of the late Coalition Government[1] and implied in the programmes of the main political parties. An active and vigilant public opinion is required if such professions of responsibility are to be carried into effect. It is a shocking thing that able-bodied willing workers should have to stand idle in large numbers; if the enforced idleness is prolonged their lives and those of their families are blighted. Of course, we cannot have everything. Not all our wisdom can dispense British people from having to endure grievous hardships from time to time. But there is a widespread feeling, which we share, that we have now reached a level of affluence, of organization and of control over our destinies, at which the evil of large-scale unemployment should be regarded as intolerable. There is a feeling that the Governments of this country before the war were culpably complacent in the presence of the amount of unemployment that existed, that they should have been much more active and insistent in their search for remedies. When it is said that the unemployment was a blot and a disgrace, these words should not be taken as a mere rhetorical flourish, but literally. It was disgraceful that responsible persons of education and culture were not so deeply shocked at the spectacle of wasted lives, as to be stirred out of their relative apathy on this issue. And if public opinion has now become rather

[1] Cmd. 6527, 1944.

clamant, if righteous indignation is burning fiercely, that is healthy manifestation.

We do not think that Professor Fisher would deny this. His fear of false and misguided remedies, that may cause greater ills than they cure, is so lively that it may hide from view his appreciation of the evil of unemployment. It is important that we should not have wrong remedies and this volume seems to be most valuable in drawing attention to the danger that we may do so.

The second proposition is that the analysis of our system made in recent years by economic thinkers, notably by Lord Keynes, points to remedies for unemployment which would avoid the pitfalls indicated by Professor Fisher, and on which we may reasonably build high hopes for a great improvement in this regard. Here, perhaps, Professor Fisher is more sceptical, or, anyhow, more cautious, and to that extent this note may be regarded as one of dissent.

This is not the place to describe the analysis made by these thinkers nor the remedies suggested by it. It suffices to say that an explanation is offered why insufficient purchasing power comes forward for the purpose of goods, and how by action at the centre this purchasing power could be increased. A remedy on those lines would not have the effect, feared by Professor Fisher, of making our structure more rigid. Rather the contrary. If the total flow of purchasing power is sufficient, the temptation to shore up unsound structures merely as a contribution to employment will be reduced; if the failure of demand in one quarter is balanced by an increase in some other, labour and capital should flow more easily to new occupations than ever before. Pleas for protecting or salvaging unprofitable production can be more ruthlessly rejected.

The underlying distrust of "full" employment policies seems to be due in part to insufficient distinction between structural unemployment and unemployment due to a deficiency of effective demand. It is the latter problem which forms the main target of modern employment policy, and we think that Professor Fisher has failed to appreciate the potential benefits, both internal and international, to be gained from policies devoted to maintaining effective demand. As far as the internal situation is concerned, Professor Fisher's concern about the deleterious effects of "full" employment on the standard of living seems to be due mainly to his imputing to the idea of "full" employment policy in general certain specific types of measure. To ensure against general unemployment due to a deficiency of effective demand requires simply that the total volume of spending shall be on an adequate level. Professor Fisher's doubts concerning "full" employment policy are largely aroused by particular types of expenditure. For instance, he thinks the elector would object to "communal expenditure in large part determined for him according to principles of 'social priority'" being substituted for "the ordinary things which he was formerly able to buy." But this has nothing to do with "full" employment policy. If Professor Fisher or the elector prefers it, any additional spending needed can be undertaken by the "electors" themselves (aided by tax remission) instead of by the central Government on objects of "social priority". This is a matter of social policy, not of full employment policy.

Professor Fisher rightly says that "the means chosen to-day for the organization of additional employment are a factor directly relevant to the level of national income to be attained to-morrow. One choice might facilitate the enjoyment of the benefits of greater productivity . . . while another might condemn us to a level of income substantially lower." This is partly a matter of the rate of investment or disinvestment, and has to do not with the amount of resources employed, but with the way in which they are used. It seems reasonable to assume that the more resources are employed, the higher the rate of investment, and hence the national income to be attained to-morrow, is likely to be.

Apart from his doubts about the internal benefits to be attained from a "full" employment policy, we feel that Professor Fisher tends to exaggerate the degree to which the effort to attain "full" employment is likely to "impede the evolution of satisfactory international economic relations". He points to the imposition of trade barriers in the nineteen-thirties introduced in the name of employment policy as a form of "full" employment policy inimical to a stable international order. This is perfectly true, but the remedy is not to abandon "full" employment as an objective, but to adopt true instead of false employment policies. The essence of modern employment policy is control of the total level of spending; diversion of spending from one country to another merely shifts the burden of unemployment, but cannot remedy a situation of general deficiency of demand. As far as the growth of trade barriers in the thirties is concerned, it was in most cases the failure to adopt true full employment policies in some important countries which led to balance of payments difficulties in others, and these difficulties were mainly responsible for the growth of restrictions on international trade.

In considering the effect of employment policies on the international economic system, it is necessary again to distinguish between policies directed against structural unemployment and those aimed at maintaining the general level of demand. The first kind of employment policy may take the form of (a) policies designed to increase mobility of labour, etc., which clearly make it easier for the country concerned to face the adjustments required by an open international economy, or (b) policies designed to freeze the existing occupational structure or to permit it to change only at a regulated pace. It is the pursuit of the second type of policy that makes it difficult for countries to participate fully in any international economic order; and it is of this kind of employment policy that Professor Fisher is chiefly suspicious.

The second and main type of employment policy, that directed towards maintaining purchasing power, tends to assist in adaptation to external changes by promoting internal mobility, apart from the fact that it avoids imposing unnecessary adjustments on other countries.

Enthusiasm for a "full" employment policy has probably been appreciably increased by the general, albeit very sketchy, knowledge that economists have recently made some contribution tending to make such a policy more practicable. But it must be confessed that many plans popularly canvassed, so far from being based on that contribution, run directly counter to it. To this extent Professor Fisher's alarm may be accounted for.

It is all a question of the right emphasis. Professor Fisher argues that in our enthusiasm for new ideas we should not neglect the truth embodied in the old. That is so, and the danger is a real one. It is also important that we should understand precisely what the new ideas are. It is important that it should not be supposed that, because we reject the old notion that our system tends in some automatic way to move to a "full" employment position in the long run, economists have given carte blanche for the adoption of any schemes, however uneconomic, that give employment in the short run. The old doctrine that uneconomic employment is unjustified stands. Protection given to it will reduce the standard of living.

In seeking a remedy for the public confusion of mind, Professor Fisher stresses the old doctrines. That is valuable. It may be still more important to get wider diffusion of a proper understanding of what the new doctrines really amount to. If that is so, the enthusiasm of their exponents should not be discouraged.

SUPPLEMENTARY NOTE

SOME members of the Group, while agreeing with the preceding comment, feel that there is still another difference of emphasis between their attitude and that of Professor Fisher.

Professor Fisher comes out strongly in favour of an open international economic system. Two main arguments have been advanced against such a system. In the first place, it has an inherent tendency towards instability, in that economic disturbances arising in any part of the system tend to be generalized. Secondly, the erection of tariffs in such a system, which have been found to be a necessary pre-requisite for the development of industries in backward countries, tends to favour unduly the large and populous political states at the expense of the smaller countries which are deprived of the benefits of large-scale production.

To meet the first difficulty—the tendency for depressions to spread internationally—it is admitted that an intelligent application of the scarce currency clause in the Bretton Woods Agreement would operate as an important mitigating influence. Nevertheless, while this provision might assist in the maintenance of the total *volume* of effective demand, it could not prevent sudden and disturbing shifts in the *nature* of that demand, to which modern economies would find great difficulty in adjusting themselves.

But the second argument is a more serious and fundamental one. Once the departure from absolutely free trade is admitted —and no realistic person could deny that some forms of protection are not only inevitable but often beneficial to the countries concerned—an open international order can no longer be regarded as a non-discriminating system. To exclude all forms of reciprocal arrangements between smaller countries which would enable them to reap some of the benefits of large-scale production enjoyed by industries and inhabitants of the large "continental" political units, constitutes a serious disadvantage for the smaller countries, against which they may have no guarantee of any offsetting advantages from the operation of the open international order as understood and advocated by the United States and Professor Fisher.

This country, in particular, as Professor Fisher himself emphasizes, is peculiarly dependent upon imports. While a well-regulated open international system along the Bretton Woods lines might conceivably succeed in establishing equilibrium in international balances of payments, it offers no guarantee that this equilibrium will be established at a level of international trade high enough to maintain the British standard of life. The need, admitted by Professor Fisher, for a high volume of international trade, is no argument for an unplanned as opposed to a planned system of international trade. Indeed, the general reduction of the risks of international trade, and the possibility of planning the development of backward areas in such a way that their industrialization plans are complementary rather than competing, all tend to suggest that a planned system of international trade could tend to lead to a larger volume of trade than an unplanned system.

None the less, it must be agreed that an open international economic system can provide a code of international economic behaviour, in fact it seems to be the only code acceptable to the United States. Since even an imperfect code may be better than none, this fact may constitute an argument in favour of an open economic system. At the same time it seems that Professor Fisher treats a *ritual* which would be valuable even if its assertions did not stand up to objective examination, as if it were a true *dogma*.

INDEX